The Way Baseball Works

The Way Baseball Works

INTRODUCED BY TIM McCARVER

TEXT BY DAN GUTMAN

A Byron Preiss/Richard Ballantine Book

NATIONAL
★ ★ ★
BASEBALL
HALL OF FAME

PRODUCED IN CONJUNCTION WITH
THE NATIONAL BASEBALL HALL OF FAME

SIMON & SCHUSTER
Rockefeller Center
1230 Avenue of the Americas
New York, NY 10020

Designed by Jeff Christensen

Editor: Dinah Dunn
Assistant Editor: Heather Moehn

Special thanks to all of the staff at
the National Baseball Hall of Fame and Museum and
Allen St. John for his additional writing and research on Chapter 5.

Manufactured in the United States of America.

10 9 8 7 6 5 4 3 2 1

Library of Congress Cataloging-in-Publication Data is available.

ISBN 0-684-81606-7

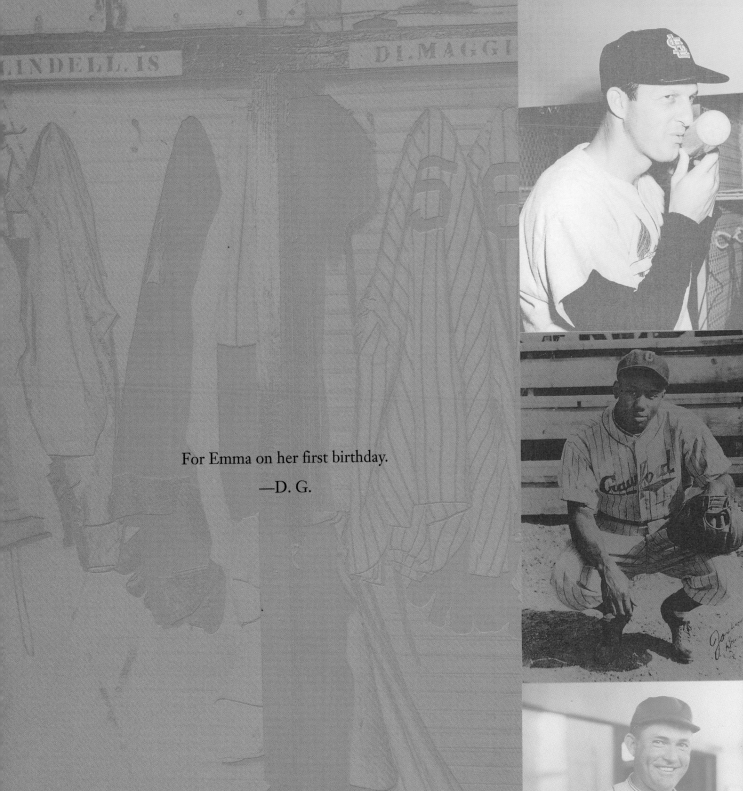

For Emma on her first birthday.

—D. G.

Table of *Contents*

Introduction by **Tim McCarver**

John Lowenstein, the one-time

baseball player and full-time character, once observed that "if Abner Doubleday had laid out the baselines at either 89 feet or 91 feet, then there wouldn't be so many close plays at first base." Lowenstein may have mixed up Doubleday with Alexander Cartwright, and reached a conclusion that defied logic if not physics, but in his own funny way, he was echoing legendary sportswriter Red Smith, who rhapsodized, "Ninety feet between bases is the nearest to perfection that man has yet achieved."

How did the game's pioneers know that if the baselines had been 89 feet or an even 100 feet that the timing of both throws and base running would be cockeyed? Or that for the batter-pitcher confrontation to be ideal, the pitcher should stand, as was determined in 1893, exactly 60 feet 6 inches from home plate? And how did they sell the American public on a game in which the defense holds the ball at the beginning of each play and the offense never lays a finger on it; the batter is pitted against nine defenders and must hit a little round ball "squarely" with a long piece of wood that has a rounded surface; the base runner must travel 360 feet along four straight, connecting baselines only to return to the exact spot he started from, as if he'd been running in circles; and the four infielders—including something called a shortstop—cover only three bases while only three outfielders cover an area as big as a landing strip? And how could they find a player in all of America who would be willing to spend the entire game in a deep crouch in foul territory, facing the opposite direction of his eight teammates and wearing a mask and other gear to prevent serious injury from fastballs and flashing spikes?

Alexander Joy Cartwright

Harry Wright

It is truly amazing that such a peculiarly conceived game, with some of the oddest rules and strategies imaginable, does indeed *work*, as the title of this book implies, and in fact works to near perfection.

Its very-public labor problems aside, baseball runs so smoothly *on* the field that many spectators begrudge today's players for receiving high salaries for playing what seems to be the least demanding of the professional sports. Certainly, players from the past perpetuated the game's easy-to-play image. Warren Spahn summed up baseball this way: "Hitting is timing, pitching is upsetting timing." Steve Carlton defined pitching as being no more than "an elevated game of catch between the pitcher and receiver." And just as Carlton ignored the batter, Hank Aaron made light of his chief nemesis, "The pitcher only had a ball, I had a bat."

Warren Spahn

Great players do make the game look so easy that the average fan can't fathom how difficult it is to play successfully. It's hard to appreciate that the game's stars play it so "easily" only after they have found ways to simplify its many intricacies. By the time they take the field, they have spent countless hours preparing themselves for every possible situation so that they can just react, letting their reflexes and athletic ability take over. Once a play is underway, it is too late to figure out what to do, which is why Jim Kaat theorized, in a very simple way, "Think long, you think wrong." The "smart," educated player automatically will take the best options on the most complicated plays.

Baseball is as much mental preparation as it is physical action, and that's why it isn't so easy to grasp by fans *or* players. It is, contended Wes Westrum, "like church. Many attend, but few understand." Even Albert Einstein couldn't comprehend this game with an infinite number of situations and results, telling intellectual catcher Moe Berg, "You'll learn mathematics before I learn baseball."

Even an Einstein has trouble understanding the "invisible" part of baseball. The average fan isn't aware, for instance, that a seemingly innocuous play early in the game may have great impact on what happens later on. For example, each "uneventful" walk or error will allow one batter an extra time at bat—and one of those batters could drive in the winning run in the ninth inning. This fan might be interested in knowing that throughout the game, the pitcher and catcher aren't simply trying to get out one batter at a time, but are "manipulating" the opposing lineup so that the best hitters come to the plate when they can do the least damage, preferably with nobody in scoring position. Sandy Koufax always would bear down on the eighth place hitter with two men out because he wanted the weaker-hitting opposing pitcher to lead off the next inning instead of the top man in the lineup. While getting the last out in one inning he was orchestrating the all-important first out in the next inning.

Sandy Koufax

The average fan also doesn't realize that some pitches are not meant to get a batter out but to set up another pitch that will. For example, inside pitches keep intimidated batters from reaching for pitches on the outside corner, even if they have two strikes against them. And the average fan might not understand that the "bad" baserunners aren't necessarily the players who are thrown out trying for an extra base but the ones who are too timid to take such chances. Or that the fielders with the most errors are often the ones who reach the most flies or grounders and risk making the most difficult throws. Unfortunately, these and many other basic concepts haven't been learned by the average player, either.

Of course, managers and coaches also aren't immune from

John McGraw

A bus interior

making costly errors in commission and omission. Too often their strategy is based on what has always been done rather than on what will work. In many cases, the strategy is outdated. I prefer the innovative manager. I'm reminded of Joe Morgan, the former Red Sox manager, back when we played together in the minors. He was a third baseman then, and told me what he planned to do some day if he were hit a slow grounder by a fast right-handed batter with two outs and a man on second. He intended to fake a throw to first and then just turn and tag the runner who was comfortably making too wide a turn around third. It was an original idea, and finally one day, he got to put it into action. It worked! It's a pity that the average fan can't also see the wheels turning in the heads of all the participants on the field. Almost everything that happens on the field is the result of choices being made on how to achieve certain results.

As above, I often think back to my days in the minor leagues because I learned so much about baseball and life when I played in the Cardinals system, beginning when I was only 17 in 1959. I think it fitting that *The Way Baseball Works* includes a section on the minor leagues because without exception, a player's time down on the farm is a formative period in his career, his rite of passage. That's when he is away from home for the first time, pulling in a salary, paying his rent, budgeting his meal money, palling around with young men from different backgrounds, and getting a glimpse of America. He grows up quickly. As much as the games, I remember playing hearts for hours at a time; devouring sandwiches that somehow had absorbed pine tar, resin, and beer; and cow-milking and cow-pie-tossing promotions at the ballparks. I also remember those endless rides on America's highways and backroads that still make me reluctant to climb aboard a bus.

The Way Baseball Works covers other topics that many fans wrongly assume have trivial importance. Take, for instance, *equipment*, the subject of the first chapter. Fans tend to take it for granted, but believe me, bats, gloves, hats, shoes, uniforms, and in my case, catching gear are the lifeline of ballplayers. Throughout the book, I talk about the importance of bats, gloves, and uniforms.

When I started catching, the chest protector had a seam down the middle, so as an unintended consequence, a ball that struck it would carom to the right or left. It took the manufacturers awhile to figure out how to change the protector's configuration so that the ball would stay in front of us. They also improved the padding, but not before I had my share of deep bruising. There's a photo in this book of the throat protector first used by Steve Yeager, and that's something I wish I had been wearing in 1979 when I was struck in the Adam's apple by a spinning breaking ball thrown by Steve Carlton. Though I had broken bones and was struck several times by foul balls in my career, nothing hurt so badly. I developed a blood clot on my vocal chord and had to spend time in the hospital, while they contemplated a terrifying-sounding operation. Afterward, I had a steel attachment welded onto the bottom of my mask for protection.

As I gained experience in the big leagues, I tried to think along with my pitchers and in doing so learned how I should approach each at bat when I was the hitter. There's a photo in Chapter Three of Steve Carlton and me on the mound, and you may be wondering what I would be telling him. Young catchers who have an annoying tendency to visit the mound at any sign of trouble should take note that the only reason Carlton listened to me was because my visits were infrequent and I would discuss only one thing each time, usually the pitch that was working

Roger Bresnahan

best. You will notice that there's no photo of me visiting Bob Gibson, and that's probably because he used to shoo me away before I reached the mound, suggesting that "The only thing you know about pitching is that it's hard to hit."

Despite what Gibson thought, my wearing "the tools of *intelligence*" allowed me to learn about pitchers and what and how they threw. In fact, Gibson, when he posted a 1.12 ERA in 1968, had the most devastating fastball I ever caught and that includes Tom Seaver, who made my gloved hand sting and swell at the 1967 All-Star Game. Gibson's fastball exploded in the strike zone. That year, he also exhibited the best control I ever saw. At will, he could throw both his fastball and slider into a circumference about the size of two baseballs on the outside part of the plate to right-handed batters. I discuss other impressive pitchers in Chapter Two of this book.

Bob Gibson

I admired the guys who knew how to play the game, like Dick Groat, who was the National League's MVP with Pittsburgh in 1960. In 1963, Groat was a Cardinal when I came up to the team to stay and he taught me a lot about baseball. As a hitter, nobody was better at the hit-and-run because he had both superb bat control and knew the best pitch-count on which to try the play in every situation. Moreover, although Groat was slow afoot, he had such great anticipation that he was an outstanding base runner and was always in position to make the play at shortstop. Groat's second base partner with the Pirates had been Bill Mazeroski, who wore a glove that barely covered his hand. When Maz, a perennial Gold Glover, later teamed with Gene Alley, they formed the best double play combination in my day. Alley had great range and made strong throws from the hole and Mazeroski had hands so quick that it often didn't look like the ball touched the leather. And Maz would stick out his thick left leg and dare runners to try to take him out before the throw—it was like sliding into a tree trunk.

In Chapter Two, Dan Gutman creates the "ultimate ball-player" by combining the best attributes of various superstars. You can't do better than by starting with Ted Williams' eyesight, which he carefully maintained, going so far as to refuse to enter dark theaters to watch movies, and Roberto Clemente's arm, a cannon he'd use to throw one-hoppers from the fence to home plate. If I had to select one individual who didn't have to borrow any attributes from any other player, it would be Willie Mays. I didn't play against Joe DiMaggio, but Mays was the best all-around player of my day, the most dangerous clutch hitter, the best curve ball hitter, and undoubtedly, the best base runner *ever*—you couldn't get any better. If anyone equaled Mays in center field it was my Cardinals' teammate Curt Flood and the Orioles' Paul Blair. One time at Wrigley Field, Curt literally used the vines to climb the wall and then he picked the ball out of them as if it were a bunch of grapes! Other than Mays' back-to-the-plate catch against Vic Wertz in the 1954 World Series, that was the greatest catch I ever saw.

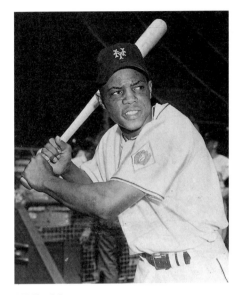

Willie Mays

But baseball is about so much more than great players making great plays. It is about practice and coaching; statistics, signs, and strategies; and choices on everything from what pitch to throw to what bat to use, from how to slide to how to prepare yourself to pinch-hit late in the game. There is so much beneath the surface. This book disassembles baseball as if it were an expensive watch and shows all the hidden components that function together to make our National Pastime tick. It doesn't merely take you *out* to the ballgame but takes you *into* the ballgame as well. For both new and long-time baseball fans, it is a ticket to an eye-opening exploration into the many ways that baseball works.

Curt Flood

MAKING A BASEBALL • INSIDE THE BAT FACTORY

ALUMINUM BATS • FIELDING, CATCHING, AND SLIDING

GLOVES • A CENTURY OF UNIFORMS • SPIKES

PROTECTIVE EQUIPMENT • THE UMPIRE'S GEAR

THE RADAR GUN • FUNGO BATS • ROSIN • PINE TAR

BATTING DOUGHNUTS • ESSENTIAL PARAPHERNALIA

Chapter One

Al Spalding as a pitcher for the Boston Red Stockings, 1875 (left); an umpire's whisk broom (above); a catcher's mask from 1895 (below).

The tools of baseball have played an enormous—but largely uncredited—role in the way the game is played. The raised seams on the ball enables a curve to curve, a knuckleball to dance. One reason the lively ball era came about was simply because machines were developed that could wind the yarn inside the ball tightly and uniformly. The precise shape and weight of the bat helps to determine how far the ball will travel. Improvements to the glove have made the number of errors decrease dramatically during the 20th century. The catcher's mask, invented by Fred Thayer in 1876, allows catchers to move up right behind the plate and become the field generals of the game. These tools of the game—in addition to the radar gun, the nonwood bat, the pitching machine, artificial turf, and others—have made baseball the sport it is.

Clockwise from top left: Emile Kinst's 1906 banana bat patent; Ernie Lombardi, spring training, 1939; Taylor Douthit's glove; and Vince Orlando, Boston Red Sox equipment manager, 1974.

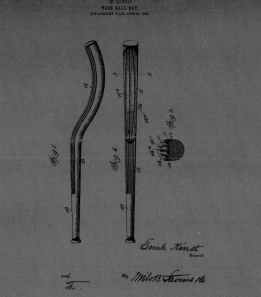

Equipment

"Any baseball is beautiful. No other small package comes as close to the ideal in design and utility. It is a perfect object for a man's hand. Pick it up and it instantly suggests its purpose; it is meant to be thrown a considerable distance—thrown hard and with precision. Its feel and heft are the beginning of the sport's crucial dimensions; if it were a fraction of an inch larger or smaller, a few centigrams heavier or lighter, the game of baseball would be utterly different."

—Roger Angell

Bob Feller

Inside **Baseball**

Like the game itself, a baseball is composed of many layers. One of the delicious joys of childhood is to take apart a baseball and examine the wonders within. You begin by removing the red cotton thread and peeling off the leather cover—which comes from the hide of a Holstein cow and has been tanned, cut, printed, and punched with holes. Beneath the cover is a thin layer of cotton string, followed by several hundred yards of woolen yarn, which makes up the bulk of the ball. Finally, in the middle is a rubber ball, or "pill," which is a little smaller than a golf ball. Slice into the rubber and you'll find the ball's heart—a cork core. The cork is from Portugal, the rubber from southeast Asia, the covers are American, and the balls are assembled in Costa Rica.

THE FIRST BASEBALL? *This battered ball was found just outside Cooperstown in the trunk of the late Abner Graves, a boyhood friend of Abner Doubleday.*

WRAP IT UP *The cotton and yarn are wound—by machine—until the ball is precisely 8.5 inches in circumference and four and one-eighth ounces without the cover. It takes a skilled worker about 15 minutes to sew on the cover by hand—108 stitches for a baseball, 88 for a softball. If you've ever wondered where the thread begins and ends, the first and last stitch are carefully tucked inside the cover.*

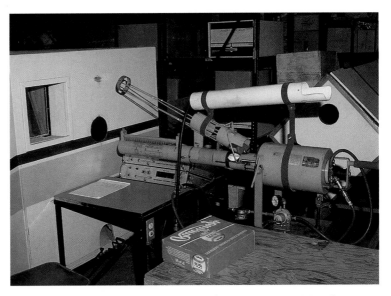

TORTURE CHAMBER *Balls are shot from a cannon at 85 mph to a wooden target. They should rebound 54.6 percent of that velocity. If a ball is more than 3.2 percent off that speed, it is rejected.*

DEAD BALL DAYS *It wasn't just the name for an era; the balls were actually called "dead." Teams would try to score in the early innings, because by the end of the game the ball would be even deader than it was in the first inning.*

"It was usually made on the spot by some boy offering up his woolen socks as an oblation, and these were raveled and wound round a bullet, a handful of strips cut from a rubber overshoe, a piece of cork, or almost anything. The winding of this ball was an art, and whoever could excel in this art was looked upon as a superior being."

—Al Spalding

THE DIRTY BALL *Before the tragic beaning of Cleveland shortstop Ray Chapman in 1920, a scuffed up, waterlogged, hard-to-see ball like this might be in action through all nine innings. Getting this kind of ball out of the game played a big part in jump-starting the home run era.*

THE COLOR LINE *Oakland A's owner Charlie Finley gave the world yellow and orange baseballs in 1973, but he wasn't the first to experiment with colors. The Brooklyn Dodgers used yellow balls for a game in 1938, shortly after night games began. Back in 1870, Peck & Snyder offered a red ball, "getting rid of the objectionable dazzling whiteness of the ordinary ball which both-ers fielders and Batsmen on a Sunny day."*

THE BALATA BALL *A shortage of rubber during World War II forced the baseball industry to search for a substitute, and a South American rubberlike gum called "balata" was chosen. It was quickly rejected when, a month into the 1943 season, the entire American League had hit only two homers. Commissioner Landis (left) ponders the situation.*

Early
Baseballs

While baseball has evolved to include night games, artificial turf, and designated hitters, the ball itself has remained remarkably unchanged for over a hundred years. Its size has been the same since 1876, the insides virtually the same since 1910. The biggest change in baseballs over the last century occurred when cowhide replaced horsehide in 1974.

AL REACH *(right) of the Philadelphia Athletics and Philly hardware-store owner Ben Shibe teamed up in 1881 to mass-produce baseballs. They sold balls of varying quality from 5¢ to $1.50. Al's son George introduced the cork-centered ball in 1911, creating the lively ball era. Al Spalding (left) bought out Reach and Shibe in 1889, but the brand name "Reach" appeared on Spalding baseballs until 1975.*

I GOT IT! *Before the 1920s, fans were required to return balls fouled into the stands. When clean, white baseballs became the rule, fans were allowed to keep foul balls, and one of baseball's most exciting traditions began.*

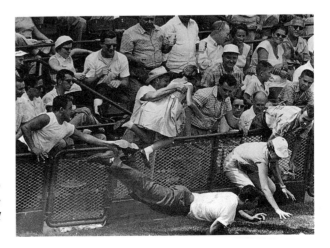

Did somebody put a **Rabbit** in that ball?

AT BATS

30
40
50
60
70
80
90
100
110
120
130
140
150
160
170
180
190
200
210
220
230
240
250
260
270
280
290
300
310
320
330

About once a decade, rumors of juiced-up balls sweep through the baseball world. The powers that be have never admitted—nor has it ever been proven—that balls have been wound more tightly to increase offense. The big jump in homers from 1909 to 1911 was a result of the new cork-centered baseball. The jump from 1919 to 1921 can be explained by the emergence of Babe Ruth and the ban on spitballs, scuffballs, and dirty baseballs. Other than that, year-to-year fluctuations may be the result of World War II, styles of hitting, expansion, quality of pitchers, size of the strike zone, development of new pitches such as the slider, and plain old random chance.

1930: 55 ABs per HR
The National League hits .303 collectively; Hack Wilson sets records with 56 home runs and 190 RBIs.

Eddie Stanky, 1948: two home runs

1920: 134 ABs per HR *Babe Ruth hits 54 home runs, and his .847 slugging average is a record that still stands. An era begins.*

1943: 94 ABs per HR *Experimenting briefly with the balata ball—a cork substitute—and HR totals plummet. The best hitters (and pitchers, for that matter) are away fighting World War II.*

1911: 160 ABs per HR *Joe Jackson hits .408 the first year of the new cork-centered ball—and still doesn't win a batting title. Ty Cobb's .420 beats him out.*

Babe Ruth, 1920

1901   **1910**   **1920**   **1930**   **1940**

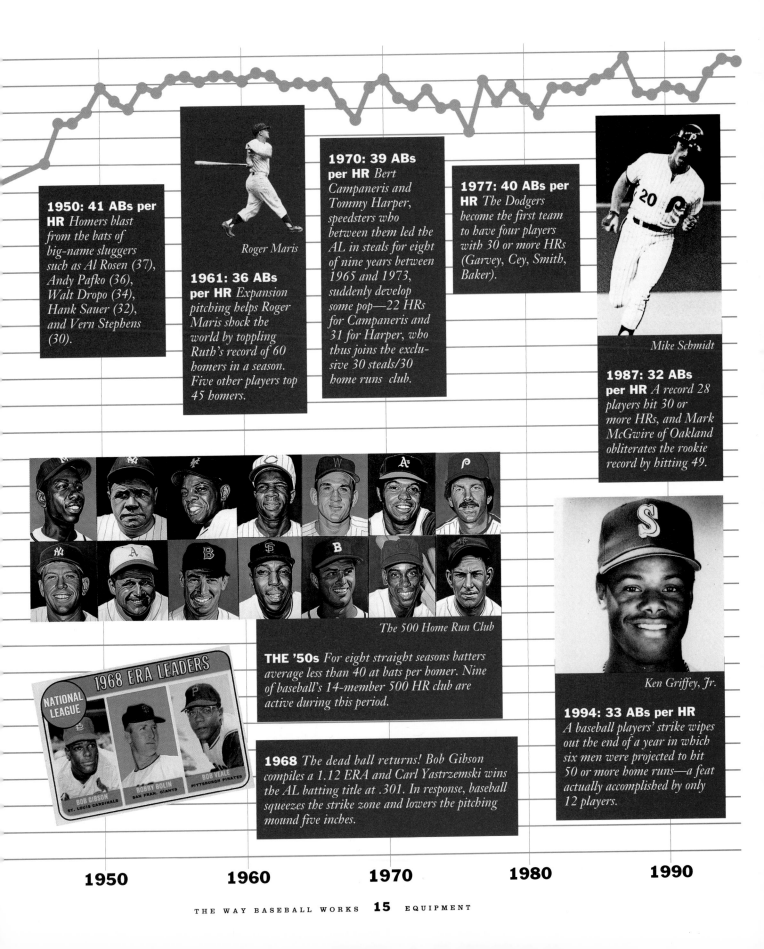

1950: 41 ABs per HR *Homers blast from the bats of big-name sluggers such as Al Rosen (37), Andy Pafko (36), Walt Dropo (34), Hank Sauer (32), and Vern Stephens (30).*

Roger Maris

1961: 36 ABs per HR *Expansion pitching helps Roger Maris shock the world by toppling Ruth's record of 60 homers in a season. Five other players top 45 homers.*

1970: 39 ABs per HR *Bert Campaneris and Tommy Harper, speedsters who between them led the AL in steals for eight of nine years between 1965 and 1973, suddenly develop some pop—22 HRs for Campaneris and 31 for Harper, who thus joins the exclusive 30 steals/30 home runs club.*

1977: 40 ABs per HR *The Dodgers become the first team to have four players with 30 or more HRs (Garvey, Cey, Smith, Baker).*

Mike Schmidt

1987: 32 ABs per HR *A record 28 players hit 30 or more HRs, and Mark McGwire of Oakland obliterates the rookie record by hitting 49.*

The 500 Home Run Club

THE '50s *For eight straight seasons batters average less than 40 at bats per homer. Nine of baseball's 14-member 500 HR club are active during this period.*

Ken Griffey, Jr.

1994: 33 ABs per HR *A baseball players' strike wipes out the end of a year in which six men were projected to hit 50 or more home runs—a feat actually accomplished by only 12 players.*

1968 ERA LEADERS

NATIONAL LEAGUE

BOB GIBSON
ST. LOUIS CARDINALS

BOBBY BOLIN
SAN FRAN. GIANTS

BOB VEALE
PITTSBURGH PIRATES

1968 *The dead ball returns! Bob Gibson compiles a 1.12 ERA and Carl Yastrzemski wins the AL batting title at .301. In response, baseball squeezes the strike zone and lowers the pitching mound five inches.*

1950

1960

1970

1980

1990

FROM BILLET TO BAT *When a white ash tree reaches 60 years old or 12 inches in diameter, it is chopped down and cut into "billets"— 40-inch cylinders. Only one out of 10 billets is good enough to produce a major league bat.*

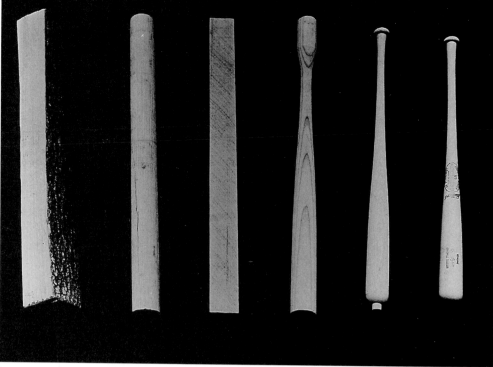

The making of a baseball bat
Good Wood

When America switched from horse-and-buggy to automobile, thousands of wagon tongues were recycled into baseball bats. Back then, they were almost as fat at the handle as they were at the barrel. Gradually, hitters slimmed down their bats. Rogers Hornsby (.424 in 1924) was one of the first to use a truly tapered bat. Until 1950, 36-ounce bats were the norm. But as fastballs get faster, so must swings. Today, in the "lite" era, 31- and 32-ounce bats are more common.

THE ORIGINAL LOUISVILLE SLUGGER *Pete Browning of the Louisville Eclipse broke his favorite bat one day in 1884. A teenager named Bud Hillerich used his father's lathe to carve Browning a new bat. Browning went three for three the next day, and Hillerich & Bradsby (salesman Frank Bradsby was made a partner in 1911) became a bat-making institution.*

AN AVERAGE TREE *will yield 60 billets. At the Hillerich & Bradsby factory in Indiana, millions of billets are aged for two years. Then they are dried, graded, and sorted by weight (two billets that are exactly the same size may be as much as 10 ounces apart in weight). Nearly all the bats are carved by machine—a lathe with 28 knives that can be adjusted to make 213 different shaped bats. H&B keeps records on every major leaguer's bat specs, down to the millimeter. It takes about 15 seconds to turn a bat. Once carved, the bat is branded, sanded, and dipped in one of six finishes. Some hitters prefer to hit with bare wood, and these bats are "roasted" briefly over an open gas flame to bring out the grain.*

GETTING A SHAVE *There are four ways to make a bat lighter. You can cut it shorter or shave wood off the barrel, both of which reduce your hitting surface. You can cork it, but that's illegal. Finally, you can shave wood off the handle, and that's what many hitters do. Bats keep getting thinner and thinner, which is one reason why you see more broken bats these days.*

Different Strokes

Cap Anson owned 500 bats, and he gave each of them a name. Babe Ruth liked to have knots in his. Eddie Collins buried his in a dunghill. Honus Wagner boiled his. Jimmy Frey soaked his in motor oil. Joe DiMaggio rubbed his with olive oil. Germany Schaefer bit his. Joe Jackson slept with his.

"Your bat is your life," Lou Brock once said. "It's your weapon. You don't want to go into battle with anything that feels less than perfect."

THE ZEBRA BAT *St. Louis Browns left fielder Leon "Goose" Goslin (below) arrived for the 1932 season with his "war club"—a bat with 12 green stripes around it. On Opening Day he walked up to the plate with it, only to have the umpires declare it to be a distraction and illegal.*

TED WILLIAMS'S BAT *The Splendid Splinter would personally go to the H&B factory in Louisville to select the wood for his bats. Williams preferred narrow-grained wood, and would drop a billet on a concrete floor and listen to the sound it made to determine if the wood was good. A perfectionist, he once returned a set of bats with a note that read, "Grip doesn't feel just right." The bats were measured and found to be .005 of an inch thinner than Williams had requested.*

SHORTEST *Wee Willie Keeler, a Hall of Famer, used a 30.5-inch bat to hit 'em where they ain't. He collected 2,947 hits and averaged .343 lifetime.*

HEAVIEST *Edd Roush (above), a Hall of Famer, lugged a 48-ounce bat to the plate from 1913 to 1931. He had a .323 lifetime batting average, but only hit 68 homers.*

WEIRDEST *Heinie Groh (above) averaged .292 over 16 seasons with his wooden "bottle bat" and hit .474 in the 1922 World Series for the New York Giants.*

LIGHTEST *Solly Hemus hit almost as many round-trippers (51) as Roush using a bat that weighed a mere 29 ounces. His best year was 1954, when he hit .304.*

The **Ping** of the bat

The dreaded nontraditional aluminum bat was introduced in 1970. The next year it was approved for Little League play and approved for college baseball in 1974. Sales of nonwood bats—aluminum, graphite, and titanium alloy—surpassed wood in 1975; today more than 75 percent of the market is non-wood.

The reason is simple. Nonwood bats last much longer and they hit a ball harder. A hollow bat is lighter, so a hitter can swing it faster. The center of gravity is closer to the hands, so the "sweet spot" is larger.

Baseball purists insist nonwood bats are dangerous to infielders, make weak hitters look better than they are, and would render 125 years of statistics meaningless.

SOFTBALL SLUGGER *Dan Schuck used a metal bat to hit 199 home runs in a single season.*

MAKING METAL BATS *starts with a round, seamless tube about 70-thousandths of an inch thick. It is pushed under high pressure through a die, and formed into the shape of a bat in a process called "swedging."*

Are we willing to hear the crack of a bat replaced by the dinky ping? Are we ready to see the Louisville Slugger replaced by the aluminum ping dinger? Is nothing sacred?

I do not want to hear about saving trees. Any tree in America would gladly give its life for the glory of a day at home plate.

I do not know if it will take a constitutional amendment to keep the baseball traditions alive, but if we forsake the great Americana of broken bat singles and pine tar, we will have certainly lost our way as a nation.

—Richard H. Durbin, *Illinois Congressman, speaking before the House of Representatives in 1989*

WILL CLARK'S BAT (*below*) *used in the 1984 Olympics. Some college players have had trouble adjusting to wood after using nonwood bats throughout their youth. Clark was definitely not one of them.*

2¾" BLACK MAGIC **EASTON** 23/4 DIA 34 IN 31 OZ. PRO BASEBALL MDL BSP BB3431

HOT HITTER *The bat is put in a 900-degree oven and plunged into a cold-water bath, which increases its strength. Foam plastic material is stuffed inside to deaden the sound. The bat is lightly sanded, buffed, printed, and the finish is applied. Finally, urethane bat caps are inserted with a pneumatic press.*

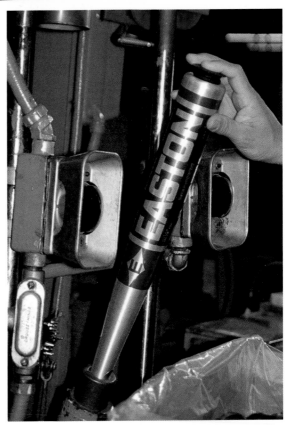

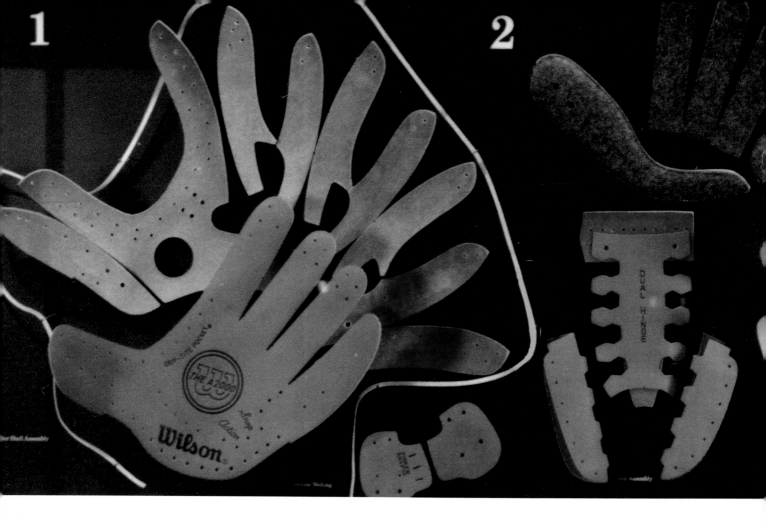

Glove *story*

At the Rawlings factory in Ava, Missouri, as many as 300 baseball gloves are manufactured every day, mostly by hand. Each glove requires about six square feet of leather—usually from a steer, because its hide is very tough. Rawlings makes 75 different models, and supplies more than half the players in the majors. One out of every three gloves that comes off the assembly line is a catcher's mitt, and one out of 12 is for left-handed fielders. From start to finish, 50 distinct steps are required to make a glove. Typically, it takes nine days to go from cowhide to glove.

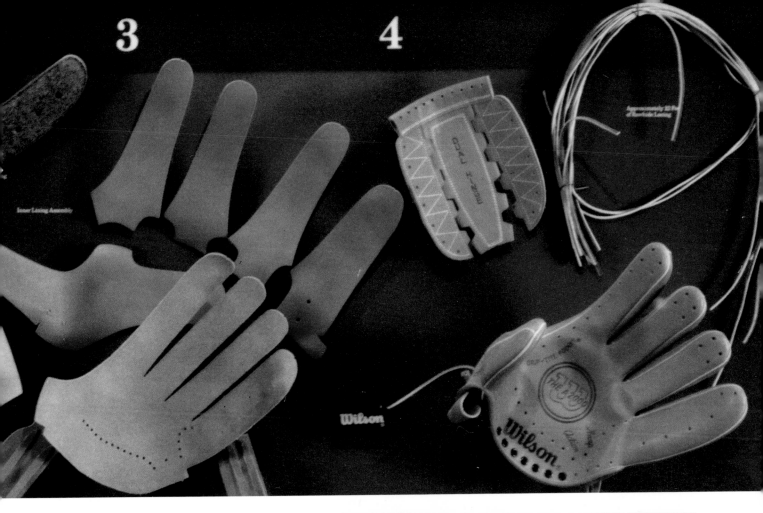

3

4

MAKING A GLOVE (SIMPLIFIED) *The cowhide is tanned, inspected, and cut into 15 to 20 pieces (above) with a device similar to a cookie cutter. The glove is stamped with a logo and model number. Then it is pounded with a mallet to form a pocket, and strips of dark blue felt are sewn onto the first three fingers. The glove is then put on an aluminum iron called a "hot hand" that shapes the fingers and smoothes the leather. Sticky wax is applied to keep the leather supple. Webbing is laced in, padding is stuffed into the heel, and the glove is ready for its final step. . . .*

SEW IT UP *It will take this worker about an hour to thread eight to ten feet of rawhide through the holes to complete the glove.*

Glove at
First Sight

LOOK, MA, NO FINGERS
Early players wore a glove on each hand. The fingers were cut off to make throwing the ball easier.

One day in 1875, a sore-handed Boston first baseman named Charles C. Waite had the audacity to appear on the field wearing a glove. Waite chose a tan work glove with an opening in the back, hoping fans and opposing players wouldn't notice. It didn't work. He was ridiculed unmercifully as a sissy. Over the next 10 years, however, baseball players realized there was nothing masculine about a handful of broken fingers. Besides, gloves improved fielding and helped win ballgames. Once pitcher/ entrepreneur Al Spalding began wearing a glove and selling gloves through his new sporting goods company, the glove took its place among baseball's essential equipment.

BAREHANDED
Louisville third baseman Jeremiah Denny, who retired in 1894, was the last position player to play without a glove.

IN THE POCKET *Bill Doak, a spitballer with the St. Louis Cardinals, came up with the idea of putting strips of leather between the thumb and first fingers of the glove to form a pocket. Fielders could then catch the ball away from the palm and make one-handed catches more easily. Doak (20-6 in 1914) patented his idea in 1922 and sold the rights to Rawlings. The "modern" baseball glove was born.*

Walter Johnson's glove

Two early gloves

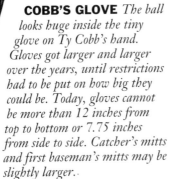

COBB'S GLOVE *The ball looks huge inside the tiny glove on Ty Cobb's hand. Gloves got larger and larger over the years, until restrictions had to be put on how big they could be. Today, gloves cannot be more than 12 inches from top to bottom or 7.75 inches from side to side. Catcher's mitts and first baseman's mitts may be slightly larger.·*

A "Trapper" Model

SPALDING
REG.U.S.PAT.OFF.
MADE IN U.S.A.

154 T

DIFFERENT POSITIONS
require different gloves. Outfielders want a big glove to reach balls over their heads. Shortstops want smaller gloves so they can get the ball out quickly. First basemen want big pockets in their gloves (right), so they can scoop up throws in the dirt.

Good **Hands**

Fielding percentage in the National League from 1880 to 1994

Muffs, miscues, flubs, and blunders used to be as common as hits, walks, and strikeouts. It was not unusual, in the early days of the game, to witness ten errors in a game or several on a single play. The art of fielding improved dramatically between 1880 and 1920. Better, bigger gloves were developed. Infields and outfields were groomed more carefully. The game itself was refined, and players became more proficient. Today, errors are less plentiful, and therefore more significant when they do occur.

1881 *Boston catcher Pop Snyder sets the mark with 99 passed balls on the year. Fellow Boston catcher Mike Hines ties it two years later.*

JUNE 14, 1876: E-4 *Boston and St. Louis combine for 40 errors in a game. Boston second baseman Andy Leonard leads the way with nine miscues.*

1928 *Taylor Douthit used this glove to corral 547 putouts, the most by an outfielder.*

1901 *Shortstop Herman Long boots his 1000th career ball, on his way to a major league record of 1076.*

THE FAMOUS.....
"BILL DOAK"
NEW IMPROVED MODEL

1919 *Bill Doak invents the pocket. Bill Gerber tops the American League with 45 errors, the first time a league leader made fewer than 50.*

1890 *In the only year of the Players League, Philadelphia's Bill Shindle mishandles 119 chances.*

1880   1890   1900   1910   1920   1930

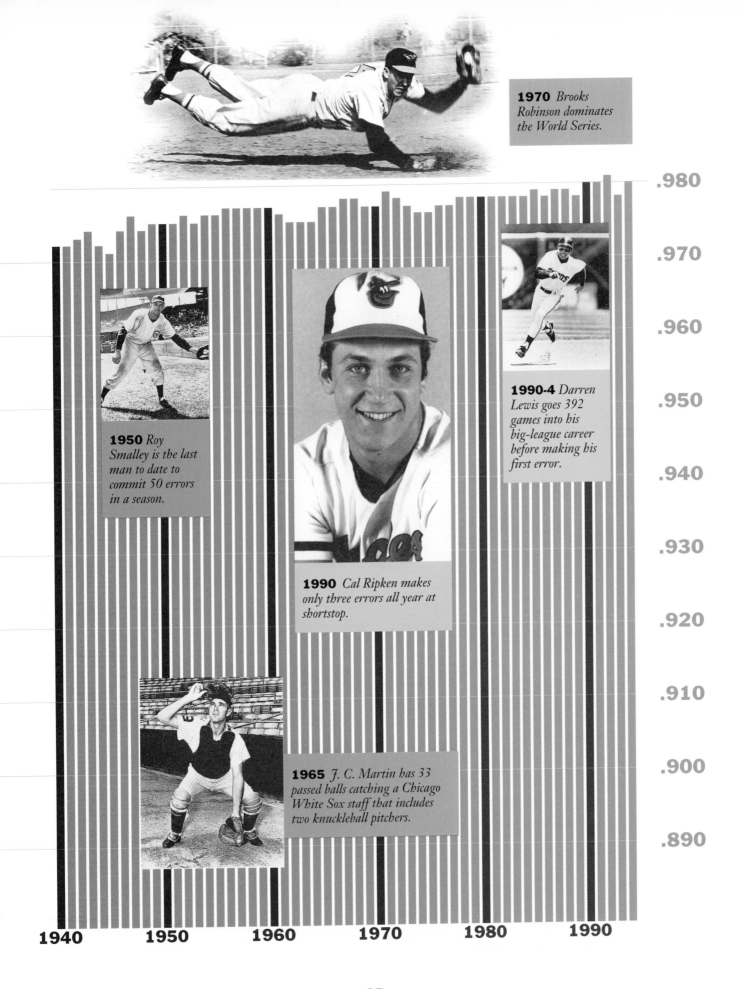

1970 *Brooks Robinson dominates the World Series.*

1950 *Roy Smalley is the last man to date to commit 50 errors in a season.*

1990-4 *Darren Lewis goes 392 games into his big-league career before making his first error.*

1990 *Cal Ripken makes only three errors all year at shortstop.*

1965 *J. C. Martin has 33 passed balls catching a Chicago White Sox staff that includes two knuckleball pitchers.*

.980
.970
.960
.950
.940
.930
.920
.910
.900
.890

1940   1950   1960   1970   1980   1990

A *century of* Uniforms

At first, baseball uniforms heralded only the name of a place—Cincinnati, Boston, Chicago, New York. Players, nearly anonymous, competed for the glory of the hometown. It was the team that mattered, not the men on it. As personalities emerged, numbers were put on their backs to assist fans in identifying individual players. But even then, the player was just a digit. Finally, the players' names appeared on their uniforms, often as prominent as team names. The individual players became what mattered. They could move from town to town freely, depending on who would pay them the most. Allegiance to the town and the team seemed almost incidental. And that, many believe, has robbed the game of its heart.

BABE'S FAREWELL *The Cleveland Indians experimented with numbers in 1916, but the Yankees were the first team to have numbers on their regular uniforms, in 1929. The numbers corresponded to the batting order. Babe Ruth hit third and wore number 3 (left). Lou Gehrig hit fourth and wore number 4. It is a myth, by the way, that the Yankees used pinstripes to disguise Ruth's weight.*

A century of **Uniforms**

SPIKES *are for traction, not for impaling infielders. Players used to buy toe and heel plates, which they would screw into their shoes (cleats). Ty Cobb denied the story that he sharpened his spikes.*

BARING SKIN *can be scary, especially when it's the muscles of Cincinnati's Ted Kluszewski (49 homers, 141 RBIs in 1954), or the legs of the 1950 Pacific Coast League Hollywood Stars (below). Spectators are used to seeing a soccer player in shorts, but they have never accepted a change in baseball attire.*

SYNTHETIC FABRICS *were developed in 1938 but were unavailable until after World War II. Baseball switched from flannel to wool and orlon in the 1960s. Charlie Finley redesigned the A's uniforms with 20-30 percent less fabric, thus removing the bagginess so common at the time. In the 1970s, cooler, lighter doubleknits came on the scene. During these decades fashion and television also changed the look of baseball uniforms.*

ITCHY WOOL *flannel was the fabric of choice for decades. Pete Reiser (above) wore it in 1941, when he became the NL's youngest batting champion, hitting .343.*

"I definitely never took my uniform for granted. Not after the summer of 1963, the year I stuck in the majors. That's when I caught 96 consecutive games, including eight doubleheaders, mostly in hot and humid St. Louis, while wearing a bulky wool uniform. Those wool uniforms could stand the wear and tear, but they weren't airy and retained your sweat. So by the end of each game, after which the trainer gave us five or six salt tablets, my wool uniform felt like it weighed more than I did."

—**Tim McCarver**

EXHIBITION GAME?
Protective gear can only help so much. A locomotive named Pete Rose barreled into Ray Fosse (left) in the 1970 All-Star Game. Fosse was never the same after this play. Shinguards and chest protector from the 1940s, cleats and mitt from the 1930s, and a 1916 mask (above).

THREE MASKS *from the beginning of the century. The catcher's mask was invented in 1876 by Frederick Winthrop Thayer, captain of the Harvard baseball team.*

The tools of
Ignorance

"We used not mattress on our hands nor cage upon our face," wrote George Ellard of the old Cincinnati Red Stockings. "We stood right up and caught the ball with courage and with grace." And mangled fingers, black eyes, bruised shins, and

broken ribs, he should have added. Slowly, sometimes reluctantly, catchers began wearing masks and mitts (1870s), chest protectors (1880s), and shin guards (1900s). Even with all that protection, people wonder why anyone with half a brain would willingly become a catcher. It was a catcher himself—Hall of Famer Bill Dickey—who dubbed the catcher's gear "the tools of ignorance." Actually, catching is the most mentally challenging position and many catchers (Connie Mack, Joe Torre, Yogi Berra) have become managers. Catcher Moe Berg (*inset*) was arguably the brightest player in baseball history.

BILLY GOAT *After a bat shattered and punctured his throat, Steve Yeager (above) popularized this neck guard.*

HARRY DECKER *designed and patented the first "modern" catcher's mitt in 1889. "The object," he wrote in his patent application, "is to provide a catcher's glove in which the padding shall be so arranged or distributed as to present greater relative thicknesses in certain determinate parts of the glove than in others." Decker, who played for Detroit, Washington, Philadelphia, and Pittsburgh, sold the rights to his mitt to Spalding. For a time, catcher's mitts were called "deckers."*

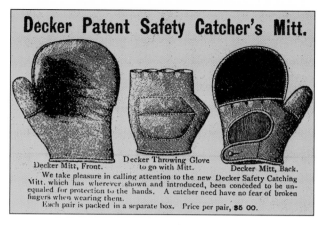

Decker Patent Safety Catcher's Mitt.

Decker Mitt, Front.   Decker Throwing Glove to go with Mitt.   Decker Mitt, Back.

We take pleasure in calling attention to the new Decker Safety Catching Mitt, which has wherever shown and introduced, been conceded to be unequaled for protection to the hands. A catcher need have no fear of broken fingers when wearing them.

Each pair is packed in a separate box.   Price per pair, $5 00.

The catcher's Mitt

On Decoration Day in 1888, Joseph Gunson of the Kansas City Blues had to catch a doubleheader even though his fingers were banged up. "I stitched together the fingers of my left-hand glove," he said. "It worked so well that I got to work, took an old paint-pot wire handle, the old flannel belts from our castoff jackets, rolled the cloth around the ends of the finger, and padded the thumb. Then I put sheepskins with the wool on it in the palm and covered it with buckskin, thus completing the mitt." By 1890, most catchers were wearing mitts.

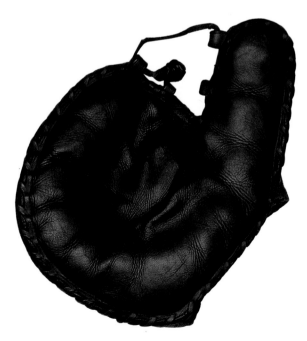

BIG BERTHA *As pitchers developed knucklers, spitters, and other baffling pitches, catcher's mitts got bigger. Hoyt Wilhelm's knuckleball was so hard to handle that Baltimore manager Paul Richards had Wilson create "Big Bertha" (right). Today, catcher's mitts cannot be larger than 38 inches in circumference.*

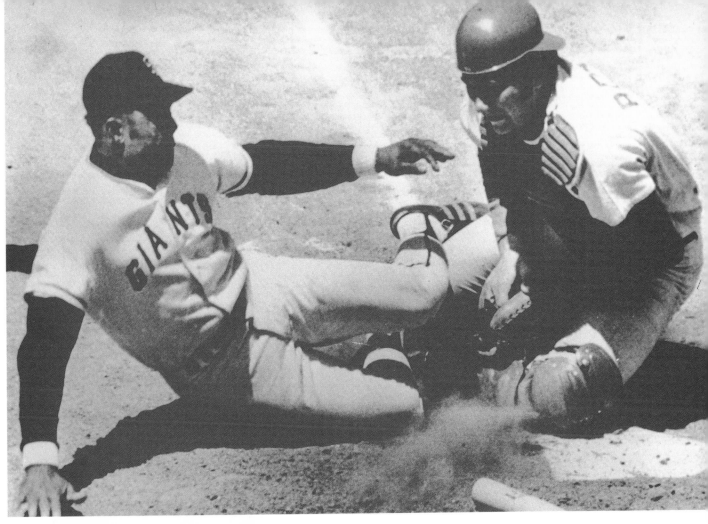

"It was the Cubs' Randy Hundley who revolutionized one-handed catching by using a mitt with a large break. It was much like a first baseman's mitt and allowed us catchers to short-hop balls, in front of us and to each side. Plus we could keep our throwing hands behind our back where they couldn't be hurt so easily. Johnny Bench and Jerry Grote became the best, trendsetting one-handed catchers of my era. I marveled at how quick their releases were."

—**Tim McCarver**

RUN AT YOUR OWN RISK *Benito Santiago (left) and Johnny Bench (above, putting the tag on Willie Mays)*

The evolution of the
Batting Helmet

It took the National Pastime more than a hundred years to realize that in a collision between a baseball and a human skull, the skull comes out the loser. The batting helmet, which became mandatory in 1971, has served to embolden the hitter, make him a little more secure in the batter's box, a little less likely to bail out on close pitches, and perhaps edge an inch or two closer to the plate. Some pitchers still head-hunt, but with the heads encased in polycarbonate alloy and thermoformed foam, they are less likely to do serious damage. Intimidation has become less of a weapon.

WILLIE WELLS *(below) is sometimes cited as the first player to wear a "modern" batting helmet. Wells was carried off the field unconscious after a beaning in 1942. Later, he visited a construction site in Newark, New Jersey, and got a worker's hard hat, which he wore the next time he came to the plate.*

1905 *The first crude batting helmet (right) was like an inflatable boxing glove wrapped around the hitter's head. "The use of my invention will not only insure the batter against injury to the head from being struck by the ball," wrote inventor Frank Mogridge in his patent application, "but will give the batter confidence and prevent him from being intimidated by the pitcher." Hall of Famer Roger Bresnahan experimented with this helmet.*

THE FLAP FLAP *Joe Rudi (above) is modeling a single-flap helmet, which became mandatory for new players in 1983. Earl Battey of the Minnesota Twins developed the first helmet with a flap. Players who reached the majors prior to 1983 are still allowed to go flapless, if they wish to. Double earflaps are now mandatory for new players.*

THEY DIDN'T CALL 'EM DODGERS FOR NOTHIN' *The Brooklyn Dodgers of the early 1940s were the first to protect their heads as a team. A Johns Hopkins brain surgeon named Walter Dandy was consulted and designed curved plastic shields that fit inconspicuously inside cloth baseball caps. Later, the team used real helmets (modeled by Gil Hodges, far left). Phil Rizzuto was the first player to wear a helmet in the American League. Brooklyn GM Branch Rickey (left) later became president of American Baseball Cap, Inc., a company that made helmets.*

"I may not look so hot in this thing, but I'd rather be alive than pretty."

—George Kell, *Detroit Tiger Hall of Famer*

EARLY HELMET *that was worn by Ralph Kiner*

BASEBALL'S FUTURE? *After getting hit by a pitch that broke his jaw in 1993, Charlie Hayes of the Colorado Rockies returned with this contraption, which is used in many Little Leagues.*

UMP WEAR *Babe Pinelli's cap, a 1922 ball, a 1948 base, Frank Umont's glasses, a brush and indicator from the 1930s (above). Umpire Bill Grieve (below) brushes off the plate and umpire Bill Kunkel (right) rubs mud on a ball to dull its surface.*

It ain't nothin' 'til **I Call It**

Umpires are in the most dangerous place in the ballpark—right behind the plate, with no mitt. Fans might remember when umpires wore enormous "balloon" chest protectors. It was "The Old Arbitrator" Bill Klem (*above*) who pioneered the inside protector. Klem took a catcher's chest protector, put on shoulder pads, and wore both of them under his shirt. He said it gave him a better look at pitches. Other National League umps followed the example, and later the American League adopted the inside chest protector.

PUGNACIOUS *George Magerkurth needed all the protection he could get. In his first game, he ejected John McGraw, and he was constantly getting into fistfights with players, managers, and even fans (right). A controversial fair/foul call in 1939 by Magerkurth led to nets being installed on the sides of foul poles.*

A MICROWAVE BEAM *shoots out of the gun, bounces off the ball in flight, and returns. The gun calculates the difference in frequency between the original wave and the reflected wave, and then translates this information into miles per hour.*

Wielding the Radar Gun

Ex-major leaguer and Michigan State baseball coach Danny Litwhiler was reading a newspaper one day in 1974 when he saw a notice about traffic cops using a "gun" to catch speeders red-handed. "I looked at it and I thought, 'I wonder if that would check a baseball?'" It did, and Litwhiler took the idea to JUGS, a pitching machine manufacturer, who adapted the radar gun for baseball. The JUGS gun quickly became standard equipment to help scouts evaluate prospects, pitchers perfect their deliveries, managers know when to yank tired starters, and broadcasters inform numbers-hungry fans.

**THE 100 MPH MEN,
according to JUGS, Inc.**

Roger Clemens

Rob Dibble

Goose Gossage

Randy Johnson

Jose Mesa

Chan Ho Park

Nolan Ryan

HOW FAST *were Bob Feller, Walter Johnson (left), and other power pitchers who played before the invention of the radar gun? We'll never know for sure. Using primitive equipment, "Rapid Robert" and "The Big Train" were clocked at around 100 mph.*

SPEED
CHECKED
BY
RADAR

ALBERT SPALDING (above) gave up a very successful pitching career (56-4 in 1875) to form the sporting goods company that still bears his name. Spalding never invented anything, but he shrewdly purchased the rights to any new device that added to the game, and he swallowed up companies that dared to compete with him.

MORTON'S Patent Sliding Pad.
A NECESSITY TO BALL PLAYERS.

The Sliding Pad protects the side and hip of the player when undertaking to slide for a base.
Its use increases a player's confidence, and renders the act of sliding free from danger.
It is worn and recommended by all leading professional ball players.
No. 0. Chamois lined, price each by mail............ $2.50
No. 1. All Canvas, price each by mail............ 1.50

TESTIMONIALS.
"I have examined and used Morton's Sliding Pad, and can say that I would not go on the ball field without one of them on, and think every ball player should have them."
M. J. KELLY, Chicago B. B. C.
"I have examined Morton's Sliding Pad, and have ordered them for our team."
CHAS. COMISKEY, Capt. St. Louis Browns B. B. C.

A. G. SPALDING & BROS.,
108 Madison St., CHICAGO. 241 Broadway, NEW YORK.

GRAND STAND CUSHION BALL GROUND

SPALDING'S BASE BALL CUSHIONS

A. G. SPALDING
108 Madison Street,
CHICAGO.

Yankee
Ingenuity

Baseball developed as a game at the same time as the Second Industrial Revolution (1875-1900). American inventors turned their talents to the National Pastime, and the United States Patent Office lists hundreds of bats, balls, and gloves, as well as pitching machines, mechanical umpires, glow-in-the-dark catcher's mitts, and inflatable batting helmets. Many of these inventions were flops, but the successful ones have made playing and watching the game more enjoyable.

SPALDING'S AUTOMATIC UMPIRE INDICATOR.

Price, 50 Cents.

SPALDING'S SHOE PLATES.

We have experienced more difficulty in the manufacture of a Shoe Plate than any other article that goes to make up a ball player's outfit, but at last we are prepared to offer something that will give the player satisfactory service.
No. 3-0. Spalding's Extra Special Hand Forged Steel Plates, polished and plated, per pair, $0.75
No. 2-0. Spalding's Hand Forged Steel Heel Plates, per pair, 50
No. 0. Spalding's Tempered Steel Shoe Plate, made of imported steel, and warranted not to bend or break; put up with screws. 50
No. 1. Professional Steel Shoe Plate, similar in shape and style to the No. 0 Plate, put up with screws............per pair 25
No. 2. Amateur Steel Shoe Plate, put up with screws........ " 15

PITCHER'S TOE PLATE.

Made of heavy brass, to be worn on the toe of the right shoe. A thorough protection to the shoe, and a valuable assistant in pitching. All professionals use them.
Each.............50c.
Any of above plates sent postpaid on receipt of price.

DANNY LITWHILER developed the radar gun, the "fly swatter" (below), and many other baseball inventions after his 11-year career as a player ended in 1951. He created a bat (right) to help players practice bunting.

THE UNBREAKABLE MIRROR *After seeing a toothpaste commercial that showed bullets bouncing off an airplane, Litwhiler went to the Pittsburgh Plate Glass Company and had them design a five-by-three-foot, 650-pound mirror that could withstand the impact of a 100-mph fastball. Pitchers use it to watch their own delivery. Litwhiler calls it "my instant movie."*

GET A GRIP *Pitchers use a cloth sack filled with sticky rosin (left) to dry their hands and grip the ball better. Hitters rub pine tar on the handle of their bats to get a good grip (right). George Brett exceeded the 18-inch pine tar limit in 1983 and hit a game-winning home run with an "illegal" bat; umpires nullified the homer. It was later restored by AL president Lee McPhail because "games should not be won and lost by technicalities."*

Essential Paraphernalia

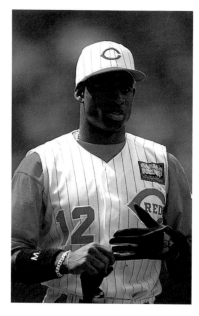

SLIDING GLOVES, *modeled here by Deion Sanders, are a recent addition to a player's arsenal. The popularity of the headfirst slide made protecting the base runner's hands necessary.*

THE DOUGHNUT, *popularized by the Yankee's Elston Howard in the 1960s, replaced the old custom of swinging two bats in the on-deck circle to make one's bat feel lighter.*

A FUNGO BAT *is longer and thinner than a regular bat. This one was used by Jimmie Reese, who was known for being able to toss the ball in the air and hit it within feet of his target. Reese broke in as a batboy in 1917, and he was still coaching until he died in 1994.*

TEED OFF *Batting tees are considered playthings for young children who aren't ready to hit a ball pitched to them. Major leaguers also use them to perfect their stroke. Before Kirk Gibson pinch-hit his dramatic homer in the 1988 World Series, he warmed up under the stands, whacking a bucket of balls off a tee.*

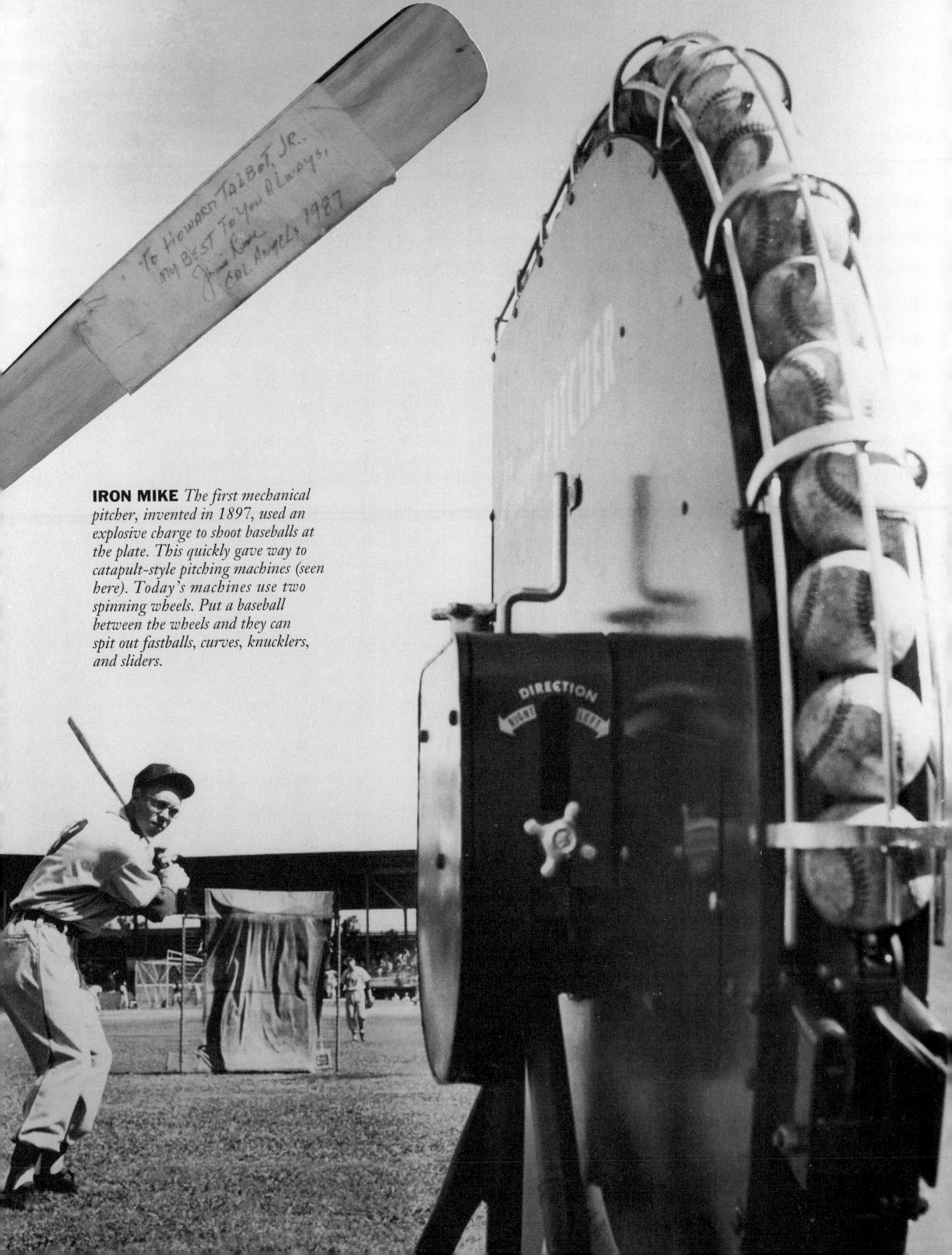

IRON MIKE *The first mechanical pitcher, invented in 1897, used an explosive charge to shoot baseballs at the plate. This quickly gave way to catapult-style pitching machines (seen here). Today's machines use two spinning wheels. Put a baseball between the wheels and they can spit out fastballs, curves, knucklers, and sliders.*

PITCHING GRIPS • SPECIAL DELIVERIES • PITCHING
MECHANICS • SPIN DOCTORS • HITTING THEORIES OF
TED WILLIAMS & CHARLIE LAU • YOUNG & OLD • THE
ULTIMATE BALLPLAYER • THE PHYSICS OF FIELDING

Chapter Two

For decades, sluggers hammered nails, tacks, and Victrola needles into their bats to make them heavier and hit farther. Then in the 1970s, they realized that bat speed was the biggest factor in hitting the long ball. Everybody switched to light bats, some going so far as to hollow their bats out illegally to lose a few more ounces.

Pitchers understand how precisely a subtle change in the way they grip the ball affects aerodynamics and the trajectory of the pitch. Hitters also tinker with the mechanics of the swing, with some endlessly obsessing over their stances.

Dozens of sports are based on one object striking another object to propel that object forward. But no other sport finds itself so interested in the science behind that collision.

A pitch in a wind tunnel (top right); Dave Stewart (right).

$$V \cdot Y)^2 \cdot \frac{(Y+1) \cdot AV}{190} + \frac{AV(Y)}{13}$$

The Science of Baseball

"Clearly, a pitcher who wished to use the drag crisis to advantage would like to be able to change the aerodynamic properties of the baseball so that different pitches could be affected by entirely different drag curves."

—**Cliff Frohlich,** *in an article in* The American Journal of Physics *entitled,* *"Aerodynamic Drag Crisis and Its Possible Effect on the Flight of Baseballs."*

$$RC = \frac{(H + BB + HBP - CS - GIDP) \cdot (TB + .26(TBB - IBB + HBP) + .52(SH + SF + SB))}{(AB + TBB + HBP + SH + SF)}$$

What makes a baseball Curve?

A baseball moves in one direction or another because of the wake of air surrounding it as it flies. If the ball were smooth, the wake would be the same on each side and the flight would only be affected by gravity. But the raised seams on the ball disrupt the wake unevenly. With one side of the ball spinning in the same direction as the air rushing by, and the other side spinning against the wind, the air becomes turbulent. There is a difference in air resistance between the two sides of the ball. According to a principle described by Swiss mathematician Daniel Bernoulli in 1738, the ball moves in the direction of least pressure, toward the direction it is spinning. The slower the pitch is thrown, the more spin can be put on the ball. And the more spin, the more curve (up to a point).

For many years, it was believed that curveballs, screwballs, sliders, and so on were merely optical illusions. But strobe photos, computer models, and wind tunnel tests have proven what hitters and pitchers have known for more than a century.

SIDEARM *deliveries (above) tilt the axis of rotation so the pitcher can give the ball a sideways spin and make it curve horizontally as it drops due to gravity. Hitters can often tell from a pitcher's grip or arm motion how the ball is going to be spinning, and therefore how it will break. That's why Nolan Ryan (left) is doing his best to conceal the ball until the last possible moment.*

"If the resistive force on a ball is proportional to the square of the velocity of the air passing the ball, it would seem probable that there would be such an unbalanced force on a spinning ball since the velocity through the air of one side of the ball at the spin equator is greater than the velocity of the other side."

—Robert K. Adair, *in* The Physics of Baseball

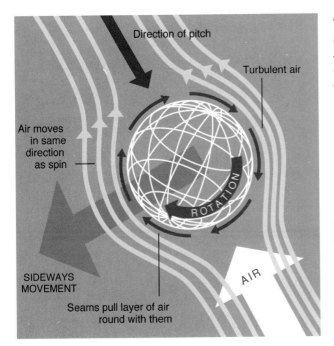

Direction of pitch

Turbulent air

Air moves in same direction as spin

ROTATION

SIDEWAYS MOVEMENT

Seams pull layer of air round with them

AIR

THE SECRETS *of the spinning baseball were first revealed by putting the ball in a wind tunnel, shooting streams of smoke past it, and watching how the smoke behaves as the ball is turned in different orientations. Today, scientists can simulate these forces with a computer.*

KNUCKLEBALLS *barely spin, so how can they curve? It was once believed that knucklers behaved erratically because they were buffeted by puffs of wind (which if true would make the pitch useless in domed stadiums). In 1975, Tulane engineers Robert Watts and Eric Sawyer performed wind tunnel experiments proving the stitches disrupted the flow of air around the ball, creating a nonsymmetrical wake. The ball, in effect, runs into a wall of air, which piles up on the stitches and pushes the ball in the other direction. Knuckleball-master Hoyt Wilhelm (above) was still throwing the pitch at age 49.*

SCUFFING THE BALL *causes an aerodynamic effect similar to that produced for a knuckleball by raised stitches. When the surface of the ball is (illegally) roughed up, the airflow around it becomes turbulent. Air resistance is increased on the side that has been altered and the ball will veer the other way. The ball is thrown so that the scuffed part stays in one place and the ball spins around it. The advantage of the scuffball over the knuckleball is that it can be thrown hard.*

Pitching **Grips**

The raised seams on a baseball give the pitcher something to grip when he delivers the ball. When the ball is in flight, the 108 stitches serve to disrupt the flow of air shooting past it. By skillfully manipulating the way he holds and releases the ball, a pitcher can throw a pitch that moves fast, slow, up, down, inside, or outside. This is the essence of pitching, the essence of baseball.

If a baseball were a smooth object like a billiard ball, the game would be totally different. Without spin, fastballs wouldn't be very fast. Because a smooth ball doesn't have seams to disrupt the airflow, there would be no curveballs, sliders, knuckleballs, screwballs, or splitters. A pitcher can't do anything to a seamless ball to make it follow a different path than the one gravity and inertia takes it on. There probably wouldn't be any home runs either, because a normal baseball hit 400 feet would only travel 300 feet if the ball were smooth.

THE FASTBALL *can be thrown with several grips. A "two-seam" fastball (above) provides the best movement. A "four-seam" fastball (below) gives the pitcher maximum velocity and can rise a few inches if thrown hard with a downward snap of the wrist and good backspin. An 85-mph fastball travels 125 feet per second. Even the fastest fastball slows down about 10 mph from pitcher to catcher, losing one mph every seven feet. Wind blowing toward or away from the pitcher can make a fastball about .7 mph faster or slower.*

THE SPLIT FINGER *fastball can be thrown hard like a regular fastball, but because the fingers are spread wide apart and not gripping the seams, the ball doesn't get much spin. Unlike a standard fastball, it sinks dramatically as it approaches the plate. The splitter was popularized in the 1980s by manager Roger Craig, but it was developed back in the 1920s as the "forkball" and used as an off-speed pitch. It requires long, strong fingers.*

THE CIRCLE CHANGE *is thrown with the index finger touching the thumb, like an "OK" sign. When the ball is jammed deep into the palm like this, it travels 8 to 10 mph slower than a fastball. A batter who is fooled by this pitch ends up swinging much too early at a ball that is traveling slower than expected. Unlike fastballs, off-speed pitches are affected dramatically by wind, especially when it's blowing across the diamond.*

THE CURVEBALL
is thrown with the middle finger pushing on the outside seam and a powerful downward snap of the wrist as the ball is released. There are many different ways to hold the ball, but a topspin or sidespin must be created so the ball will drop dramatically on the way to the plate.

THE KNUCKLEBALL *is misnamed because it is gripped with the fingertips, not the knuckles. The pitcher keeps his wrist stiff and throws the ball at about 65 mph with little or no spin. It's a difficult pitch to throw and virtually impossible to control. The ball may break two or more times in any direction on the way to the plate. "It looks like a pigeon coming out of a barn door," said Bob Feller. In order to get a better grip on the ball, some knuckleball pitchers cut their fingernails square. The pitch was perfected by Eddie Rommel back in the 1920s, and only a few others have mastered it including Hoyt Wilhelm, Wilbur Wood, Phil Niekro, Charlie Hough, Tom Candiotti, and Tim Wakefield among them.*

"The best [knuckleballer] I ever caught was St. Louis Cardinals pitcher Barney Schultz. When a batter saw there was no spin on it, he knew he was in trouble. As Charlie Lau said, 'There are two theories on hitting the knuckler. Unfortunately, neither of them works.'"

—Tim McCarver

THE SLIDER is usually gripped like a curveball, but the pitcher doesn't snap his wrist. The wrist is stiff. Upon release, he puts pressure on, or "cuts," the ball with a finger to give it sidespin like a spinning bullet. The slider release has been compared with passing a football. The pitch doesn't break as much as a curve, but it starts its break closer to the plate. Thrown by a right-hander, sliders dart away from right-handed batters and in on lefties.

THE CURVEBALL With a good wrist snap, it is possible to spin a baseball at 1,800 rpm, which means it would make about 15 revolutions on its way to the plate. According to a study by Lyman J. Briggs of the National Bureau of Standards, a baseball can curve as much as 17.5 inches and the most effective velocity is 68 mph. The human wrist is constructed so it is easier for right-handers to twist their wrists clockwise and left-handers counterclockwise. So a right-hander's curve will move away from a right-handed batter.

And when a ball breaks:

Spin Doctors

"In recent years I've noticed many pitchers falling into the habit—a bad habit—of throwing too many sliders. The slider is the easiest pitch in the world for the catcher to call for. It's comfortable to handle, and many catchers think it's a tough pitch to hit."

—Tim McCarver

CANDY CUMMINGS *is usually credited with inventing the curveball.*

THE SCREWBALL is thrown by twisting the wrist in the opposite direction it twists naturally. The pitch, therefore, curves in the opposite direction of a curveball. So a right-hander can throw a screwball when he wants a pitch that will move away from a left-handed batter. Screwballs are difficult to throw and put a lot of strain on the forearm and elbow.

CARL HUBBELL *threw so many screwballs in his 16-year career that his hand was permanently turned so that the palm faced out. "King" Carl had five straight 20-win seasons, won the MVP twice, and won 24 straight games during the 1936 and 1937 seasons. Christy Mathewson threw the "screwgie" before Hubbell, but he called it a "fadeaway." In more recent years, Fernando Valenzuela has been the master of the screwball.*

WINDUP *Left-hander Warren Spahn, who won 363 games with 20 wins in each of 13 seasons, demonstrates good pitching mechanics. If any of the following steps are even slightly off, the result will be poor control, little velocity, or a hanging curve. First, Spahn takes a small step back with his right foot and brings both hands back at the same time. This rocking is not necessary but it starts the ball in motion and prepares the body for the forward thrust toward home plate.*

LEG LIFT *With his foot back, Spahn would raise his arms over his head (not pictured). As he brings his arms down into his waist (hiding the ball from the batter), Spahn lifts—not kicks or swings—his right leg up and to the side to twist his body like a spring.*

THRUST *Spahn brings his left arm back, with his elbow leading his hand. Energy is stored in the arm's stretching tendons like a spring and transferred to the ball as the hand accelerates forward. At the same time, he is rotating his body by "exploding" his hips and striding forward on his right leg, thrusting his body weight in the same direction as the ball as he releases it. The body's momentum carries him forward, into position for fielding.*

FOLLOW-THROUGH *Upon release, he is putting about 1.5 horsepower behind the ball, which is accelerating at 40 g's, or 40 times the acceleration of gravity. As he got older, the tendons in his arm that generate this power lost some of their elasticity and he lost his overpowering fastball. To compensate, Warren Spahn turned to a slider and screwball and pitched a no-hitter five days after he turned 40. He went 23 and 7 when he was 42 and was still pitching at age 45.*

"When I'm pitching, I feel I'm down to the essentials. Two men, with one challenge between them, and what better challenge than between pitcher and hitter?"

—Warren Spahn

Special
Deliveries

Until 1893, pitchers were restricted to a 4-by-6-foot box in which they would run forward like a javelin thrower, gathering momentum for the pitch. Once the pitching rubber replaced this large box, it became necessary for pitchers to develop a "windup," essentially using the limbs of the human body to create that same momentum while keeping a foot planted in one place. The body mechanics of this windup are the keys to velocity and control.

Because body shapes and styles are different, there will never be a pitcher who has a delivery with "perfect mechanics." Tom Seaver *(right, top)* would scrape his right knee against the mound upon releasing the ball. Juan Marichal *(below Seaver)* kicked his leg high in the air. Walter Johnson barely lifted his leg at all. Hideo Nomo swivels his body around toward second base. Each of these great pitchers spent countless hours figuring out the best way to use his body to propel a baseball sixty feet and six inches.

JIM ABBOTT *was born without a right hand and had to create a unique delivery that would enable him to hold his glove and transfer it onto his throwing hand immediately after releasing the pitch. Nevertheless, Abbott became an excellent player, pitching the United States to an Olympic gold medal in 1988, winning 18 games for the Angels in 1991, and throwing a no-hitter for the Yankees in 1993.*

The pitch
Trajectory

DWIGHT GOODEN *came up to the Mets in 1984 and fanned a league-leading 276 batters in only 218 innings with his rising fastball. The next year he led the league in strikeouts again and became the first National League pitcher in the century to strike out 200 or more batters in each of his first two major league seasons.*

THE FASTBALL seems to travel horizontally, on a perfectly straight line. In fact, the pitcher must throw the ball at a slightly upward angle to avoid throwing every pitch in the dirt. All objects are powerfully attracted to the Earth by the force of gravity and fall with a constant acceleration (32 ft/sec/sec). A 100-mph fastball will drop about two feet and two inches in the approximately .4 seconds it takes to get to the plate.

JIMMY KEY has never had an overpowering fastball like Gooden, but he makes up for it with a good curve, slider, change-up, and with outstanding control. Key has never won 20 games in a season, but he has had winning seasons that any pitcher would envy: 14-6, 17-8, 12-5, 13-7, 18-6, and 17-4.

THE SLIDER is thrown harder than a curveball, but not as hard as a fastball. An 85-mph slider will drop about two feet and seven inches. The ball breaks down and sideways (the "slide" in slider) five to ten inches. It is sometimes called a "nickel curve" or "the pitch of the sixties." Steve Carlton is often credited with having the deadliest slider.

RIP SEWELL *shot off part of his foot in a hunting accident, prompting him to develop his "eephus" pitch, a lob that reached a height of 25 feet. It was difficult to hit, because it crossed the strike zone at a steep angle. Sewell threw Ted Williams three of them in a row during the 1946 All-Star Game. Williams took the first one, fouled off the second, and slammed the third over the rightfield fence. It was the only homer ever hit off Sewell's eephus.*

THE CHANGE-UP is thrown the slowest of all, about 20-mph slower than the pitcher's fastball. Naturally, it spends more time in the air than other pitches, and has a prounounced arc. No batter is ever "overpowered" by a change-up, but it is still a very effective pitch. A good change-up keeps the hitters guessing, gives the pitcher the element of surprise, and makes his fastball seem faster by comparison.

Timing the **Swing**

.00 SECONDS *The pitcher releases a pitch about 54 feet from the plate (because his arm extends in front of the rubber). An 85-mph pitch will be in the catcher's mitt in about .43 seconds. A 100-mph pitch will get there in close to .40 seconds. In any case, the hitter must already be moving his bat back before the ball is released to prepare for his swing. He is focusing on the release point, trying to see the rotation of the seams to determine the speed and location of the pitch.*

.13 SECONDS *The hitter must make his decision about whether or not he will swing, and begin bringing the bat around. The longer he waits, the more he gets to see of the pitch, but the faster he'll have to accelerate the bat if he wants to hit it.*

.20 SECONDS *When the ball is halfway to the plate, the hitter must be in the process of swinging. It will take him about .28 seconds (.23 for the greats) to accelerate the bat to a horizontal position across the plate.*

.25 SECONDS *After swing is underway for .10 seconds, it's almost impossible for the hitter to make an adjustment to it. He loses sight of the ball when it's about 10 feet away from him. That's why a pitch that breaks close to the plate is so difficult to hit.*

.40 SECONDS *The bat must be moving 76 mph at this point to hit the ball 400 feet (86 mph to hit a ball 450 feet). If the swing is .01 seconds too early or too late, the ball will go down one of the foul lines. If it's .03 seconds off, the bat hits nothing but air. If the batter times it perfectly and hits it square, the ball will come off the bat at over 100 mph.*

The physics of **Hitting**

Baseball may be a game of inches, but the science of hitting a baseball reduces the numbers down to quarter inches and milliseconds. One infallible truth is that a squarely hit ball results in a line drive. Any deviation and the results vary wildly: If the batter hits the ball three-quarters of an inch above the center, he hits a grounder; three-quarters of an inch below the center, and he's likely to hit a home run; another quarter of an inch down, and it becomes a routine fly ball; one inch lower, and it's a foul straight back; and if he's farther off than that, it's a swinging strike.

Paul Kirkpatrick, a physicist at Stanford, once looked at the position of the bat, its angular and linear momentum, timing, and so forth, and calculated that there is a finite number of variables involved in hitting a baseball. With each variable the batter can make one of two mistakes (too early or too late, too high or too low, etc.). So the batter, according to Kirkpatrick, "is faced at the outset with twenty-six roads to failure." Maybe that's why few disagree with Ted Williams's belief that hitting a baseball is the single most difficult thing to do in the sport.

KEEP YOUR EYE ON THE BALL
In fact, it is physically impossible for a hitter to actually see his bat hit the ball. He must swing at where he thinks the ball will be when it crosses the plate. The margin for error often comes down to a fraction of an inch.

WHEN THEY SAY, *"He crushed it," they're not kidding. A well-hit baseball is battered by 8,000 pounds of force, and this power compresses the ball to about one half of its original diameter.*

WILLIAMS *was so obsessed with hitting that his roommates would be startled to see him awake in the middle of the night and practice his swing in his pajamas before a mirror. It paid off. The "Splendid Splinter" finished his career with a .344 average, six batting titles, two Triple Crowns, and 521 homers despite missing nearly five years of professional play for military service.*

The hitting theories of
Ted Williams

Ted Williams may have been the best natural hitter ever, but he strongly believed that hitting could be taught. He studied the art like a scientist and even wrote a book titled *The Science of Hitting*. The Williams philosophy, in a nutshell, is that there are three rules to hitting: First, the hitter has to get a good pitch to hit. Hitting a baseball is tough enough when the pitch is over the plate, so hitters should never swing at a pitch outside the strike zone. Second, the hitter has to use his head and do his homework. He has to know the answers to questions like: What's the pitcher's best pitch? What did he throw me last time I faced him? What are my strengths and my weaknesses? What does he usually throw on the first pitch? Finally, the third rule is to be quick with the bat. As soon as the hitter makes the decision to swing, he should swing aggressively.

THE HEAD
"The hip movement is a spinning action, with the head as the axis, and it must not be restricted."

THE STRIDE
"Be careful not to overstride, because then you spread your hips and prevent a good pivot, diminishing power." The batter gets a big push off his back foot as he swings. By the time the bat crosses the plate, there is almost no weight on the back foot.

"If there is such a thing as a science in sport, hitting a baseball is it. As with any science, there are fundamentals, certain tenets of hitting every good batter or batting coach could tell you. But it is not an exact science."

—Ted Williams

THE BAT

"The flight of the ball is down, about five degrees. A slight upswing—again, led by the hips coming around and up—puts the bat flush in line with the path of the ball for a longer period."

THE STANCE

"Your weight should be balanced, distributed evenly on both feet and slightly forward on the balls of the feet, with the knees bent and flexible. The feet are good and planted, the lead foot open so as not to restrict your pivot but slightly closer to the plate than the back foot." Williams would spread his feet 27 inches apart.

Ty Cobb

THE HANDS

"I believe you feel more comfortable and can be quicker with your hands nearer the body—that is, three to eight inches." The arms and hands are used mainly to transfer the body's energy to the bat. The power of the swing actually comes from the legs and torso.

THE ARMS

"I held my bat upright, almost perpendicular to the ground."

THE HIPS

"As the hips come around, the hands follow, just as in golf, and the bat follows the hands. The way you bring your hips into the swing is directly proportional to the power you generate."

Johnny Bench

The Sweet Spot

is a bat's "center of percussion," and is located six to eight inches from the end. When you hit a ball at that point, the impact feels effortless and your hands don't sting at all. To find the sweet spot on a bat, hold it by the knob and tap it up and down with a hammer. When you don't feel a vibration, the spot you're tapping is the sweet spot. Nonwood bats have a larger sweet spot because they are hollow and the weight is more evenly distributed. Nonwood bats hit balls about four mph faster than wood bats, which translates to a 10 percent increase in distance.

The **Lau/Hriniak** *school of hitting*

While Ted Williams used his success to teach hitters what to do, Charlie Lau used his lack of success to teach hitters what *not* to do.

Lau was a reserve catcher hitting .180 for the Orioles in 1962 when he decided to try a new philosophy of hitting. He adopted a wide stance, like spray hitters before the home run era. He held his bat almost parallel to the ground. He decided to go for slashing liners and hard grounders, using the entire field, hitting outside pitches the other way. In other words, he stopped trying to hit home runs.

Lau's average zoomed to .294. When he retired from active play and became a batting coach, he taught his system to the Orioles, A's, Royals, Yankees, and White Sox, and they all won titles. Lau's book, *How to Hit .300*, became the "bible of batting" and he became a guru to stars such as Hal McRae, Amos Otis, Wade Boggs, Carlton Fisk, Don Mattingly, and George Brett.

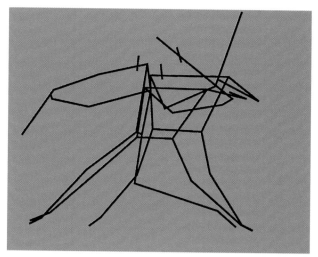

LAU WAS ONE *of the first to use videotape to help hitters discover flaws in their mechanics. Now a number of companies take videos of athletes and turn them into stick figures so they can analyze their swing by computer.*

GARY REDUS *(right) hit 17 homers as a rookie with the Reds in 1983. He was a notorious low ball/fly ball hitter. "The head leads the body," says Lau. "Wherever you turn your head, the rest of your body—your shoulders, arms, hips, and everything else—follows."*

SADAHARU OH *(left) won 13 home run titles and slammed 868 dingers in Japan with his distinctive foot-in-the-air stance. According to Lau: "A good hitter brings the bat to the position where his hands are back, with the top hand at about upper-chest level and just off the rear tip of his shoulder. The bat is held above his rear shoulder at about a 45 degree angle. And that's where it is at the moment his front foot hits the ground."*

WHILE CHARLIE LAU (far left) died in 1985, his hitting philosophy has been carried on by his disciple Walt Hriniak (left). Lau had managed Hriniak in the minors and inspired him to become a hitting instructor. Hriniak was another poor hitter who embodied the maxim, "Those who can't—teach." He had 99 major league at bats in his career and got 25 hits, all singles.

READY . . . *George Brett of the Kansas City Royals was a mediocre hitter until Charlie Lau taught him to stop waiting for fastballs he could hit over the fence. "To be truly balanced in your stance," Lau advised, "you must have your feet set apart, your knees flexed, and your body bent slightly at the waist." Lau compared a hitter's stance to building a house. You have to start with a firm foundation.*

AIM . . . FIRE! *"You should start the actual swing of the bat from a firm front side with your hips closed. Then, at the instant of contact, you should open your hips so the power they generate can aid the swing at the moment it will do the most good, and that is when the power of your arms is at its greatest." Brett is about to release his top hand from the bat, which Lau suggested hitters do to get good extension of the arms and a strong follow-through.*

Ages and **Stages**

Youth is wasted on the young, they say. The male body usually reaches full maturity by the age of 20. A typical rookie comes up to the majors a year or two later with a lot of raw talent. After he gets a a few years of experience, he's likely to have his "career year" before he turns 30. After that, his reflexes slow, his weight goes up, he loses a few steps, injuries nag him, and his numbers begin to tail off. His accumulated wisdom helps put off the inevitable for a few years, but it is a rare ballplayer who can still achieve greatness as he approaches his 40th birthday. The chart below shows what some players have accomplished at specific ages.

■ **AGE 15:** *Joe Nuxhall of the Cincinnati Reds becomes the youngest player of the 20th century to play in the majors.*

■ **AGE 28:** *Rogers Hornsby (left) hits .424, the highest average in the 20th century. Jackie Robinson is a rookie. Steve Carlton wins 27 games.*

■ **AGE 31:** *Sandy Koufax retires because of an arthritic pitching elbow. Joe Jackson banned for life.*

■ **AGE 20:** *Tony Conigliaro leads the American League with 32 homers.*

■ **AGE 17:** *Mel Ott reaches the majors. Bob Feller fans 17 batters in a game.*

■ **AGE 22:** *Walter Johnson goes 25-17 and strikes out 313.*

■ **AGE 24:** *Dizzy Dean wins 30 games. Denny McLain wins 31. Jose Canseco forms the 40-40 club. Frank Thomas hits 46 homers with 122 R.B.I.s.*

■ **AGE 29:** *Randy Johnson leads the league in strikeouts for the first time.*

17 18 19 20 21 22 23 24 25 26 27 28 29 30 31 3

■ **AGE 19:** *Dwight Gooden strikes out 276 in a season.*

■ **AGE 21:** *Ken Griffey Jr. hits .327.*

■ **AGE 25:** *Babe Ruth gives up pitching to play every day. Ty Cobb hits .420, his highest average. Mickey Mantle wins the Triple Crown.*

■ **AGE 27:** *Joe DiMaggio hits in 56 consecutive games. Hank Greenburg hits 58 homers. Don Larsen pitches a perfect game in the World Series. Roger Maris hits 61 homers. George Brett hits .390.*

■ **AGE 30:** *Hack Wilson (left) drives in 190 runs. Maury Wills swipes 104 bases. Wade Boggs wins the last of his five batting titles.*

■ **AGE 23:** *Christy Mathewson (left) wins 30 games for the first of three straight seasons. Ted Williams hits .406. Johnny Vander Meer pitches back-to-back no-hitters. Rickey Henderson steals 130 bases.*

■ **AGE 26:** *Babe Ruth hits 59 homers. Nolan Ryan pitches his first no-hitter.*

■ **AGE 35:** *Cal Ripkin Jr. tops Lou Gehrig's consecutive game record; Gehrig's last full season; Lou Brock swipes 118 bases (above, left to right).*

■ **AGE 59:** *Satchel Paige (above) pitches three scoreless innings for Kansas City.*

■ **AGE 41:** *Ty Cobb gets his final hit.*

■ **AGE 38:** *Ted Williams hits .388 with 38 homers. Roberto Clemente collects his 3,000th and final hit.*

■ **AGE 42:** *Stan Musial hits .330. Warren Spahn wins 23 games. Gaylord Perry wins the Cy Young Award. Satchel Paige makes his major league debut.*

■ **AGE 33:** *Ty Cobb wins the last of his 12 batting titles. Bob Gibson goes 22-9 with 1.12 E.R.A.*

■ **AGE 37:** *Walter Johnson (above) wins 20 games for the last time.*

■ **AGE 40:** *Babe Ruth hits his 714th home run. Henry Aaron hits his 715th home run.*

■ **AGE 58:** *Minnie Minoso makes his final appearance, going 0 for 2.*

33 34 35 36 37 38 39 40 41 42 43 44 45 49 58 59

■ **AGE 34:** *Willie Mays hits 52 homers in his last .300-plus season. Harvey Haddix pitches his 12-inning "perfect" game. Tony Gwynn hits .394.*

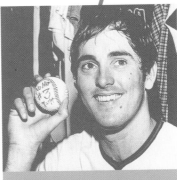

■ **AGE 49:** *Hoyt Wilhelm throws his last knuckleball.*

■ **AGE 32:** *Babe Ruth hits 60 home runs. Thurman Munson's career and life end in plane crash.*

■ **AGE 39:** *Grover Cleveland Alexander (left) strikes out Tony Lazzeri and wins the 1926 World Series for the Cardinals. Hank Aaron hits 40 homers, the most ever by a player that old.*

■ **AGE 44:** *Pete Rose tops Cobb as the all-time hit leader. Nolan Ryan (above) pitches his 7th no-hitter.*

The **Ultimate** *position player*

If we were mad scientists with an obsession to create the perfect baseball player, we would select bits and pieces of various players and combine them into one super athlete—a baseball-playing monster. The choices here are subjective, of course, but few would argue that together they would make one helluva ballplaying machine.

THE BRAIN: MOE BERG
Magna cum laude at Princeton, speaker of many languages, quiz show star, off-season lawyer, part-time spy for the U.S. government, and 15-year veteran for the Dodgers, White Sox, Indians, Senators, and Red Sox.

THE EYES: TED WILLIAMS *He had 20/10 vision and was said to be able to read a record label as it was spinning (33 1/3 rpm, that is).*

STRENGTH: FRANK HOWARD
6'8" and 275 pounds of raw power, "The Capital Punisher" once hit 10 homers in 20 at bats. Actually, Howard looked like he was already created in a laboratory.

THE ARM: ROBERTO CLEMENTE
Look up "rifle arm" in the dictionary and you'll see his picture.

THE WRISTS: HENRY AARON *They say he could wait until a pitch was virtually in the catcher's glove, and then drive it over the wall. That's how Hammerin' Hank managed to hit more home runs than any player in major league history.*

THE LEGS: RICKEY HENDERSON *Stealing bases requires more than just raw speed, but we've got to pick the man who led the American League in stolen bases 11 times, swiped 130 in 1982, and has more steals than any player in the history of the game.*

THE DRIVE: TY COBB *He burned with an intensity that has never been approached by any other player.*

STYLE: JOE DIMAGGIO *The Yankee Clipper was not only a spectacular hitter, runner, and fielder, he also played with a certain grace that has never been duplicated. Whether he was at the plate, in the field, or out in public, he made everything look easy.*

CHARISMA: BABE RUTH *He wasn't a human being, he was an alien dropped from outer space specifically for the world to have somebody to love. It just so happened that he could win 24 games in a season as a pitcher, clout 714 home runs, and hit for a .342 lifetime average.*

DURABILITY: CAL RIPKEN *The man plays one of the most demanding field positions and did not take a day off in 14 years. Nuff said.*

ENTHUSIASM: ERNIE BANKS *No player ever looked forward to coming out to the ballpark more than Banks did. Let's play two!*

REACTION TIME *is important for every fielder, but it is most crucial for infielders and could be a matter of life and death at third base. The ball usually comes off the bat faster than it left the pitcher's hand, so it gets to "the hot corner" in a fraction of a second. Second baseman Joe Morgan (right) dives for a line drive.*

The physics of
Fielding

Catching a baseball may not be quite as difficult as hitting one, but it requires good reaction time, running speed, and most importantly, the somewhat mysterious ability to judge the trajectory of a flying object. Paradoxically, it's harder to catch a ball hit directly at you than it is to catch one that you have to run toward. This is because a ball hit to the fielder's left or right allows him to see the parabolic arc of the trajectory. A ball hit right at him just appears to move up and down. Some players step to the side of a ball coming right at them to see the trajectory better. Others use the old "thunk" method: When they hear the crack of the bat, they run back. If the bat makes more of a thunk sound, they run in.

BALANCE *Infielders like Billy Martin (left) wait for the pitch in a crouch with their feet spread apart and knees bent because this position gives them great stability, a low center of gravity, and a wide base of support. They can do anything from this position—scoop up a grounder, break to either side, or leap to snare a liner if they have to.*

GROUNDERS *are hit above the middle of the ball, which gives them topspin. On artificial turf, it appears that they increase in velocity with every bounce through the infield. They don't. They just don't slow down as much as when they hit grass. Don Mattingly (above) turns a 3-6-3 double play.*

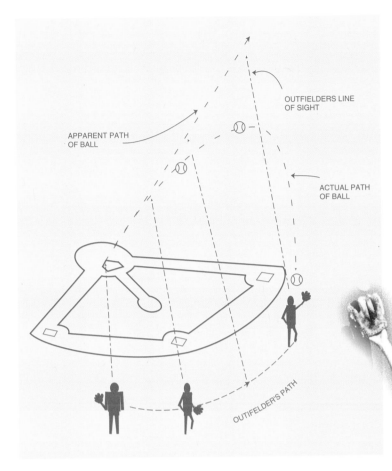

OUTFIELDERS LINE
OF SIGHT

APPARENT PATH
OF BALL

ACTUAL PATH
OF BALL

OUTIFELDER'S PATH

GETTING HIGH *Thin outfielders with long legs and powerful quadriceps (thigh) muscles are most likely to make catches like the one Joe Rudi made in the 1972 World Series (left). The key is to get a running start and a powerful push off the ground to generate high vertical launching acceleration. Swinging the arms up to catch the ball also contributes to getting height. The world high jump record is close to eight feet, but high jumpers are trying to get their entire body over a bar. Outfielders just trying to reach as high as possible can only get about 4.5 feet off the ground. Rudi makes another great grab (above), this time in the 1972 playoffs.*

"Every action is opposed by an equal and opposite reaction."

—**Isaac Newton**

IN ANY COLLISION, *Isaac Newton said, the two objects exert equal and opposite forces on each other for the same period of time. On a play at the plate, the object with the bigger mass (usually the catcher) will have his velocity changed the least after the collision. However, if the base runner has enough momentum (mass times velocity) he may drive the catcher (Carlton Fisk at left) backward.*

THE STRIKE ZONE • THE COUNT • RUNNING
THE BASES • SIGNS • FILLING OUT THE LINEUP
MANAGING A PITCHING STAFF • THE PLATOON
SYSTEM • TURNING TWO • K KORNER • HEAD
GAMES • CHEATING • BENDING THE RULES

Chapter Three

Sal Maglie, top, and Joe Rudi, above

If aliens were to visit Earth, they could probably figure out most team sports easily enough because they're simulations of warfare—one team attempts to march down the field into the other team's territory and ultimately score a goal, symbolically defeating them.

The aliens, however, would probably find baseball to be baffling. The object of the game is not obvious. Every play is influenced by an infinite number of rules, possibilities, and options. There seems to be a lot of standing around between brief bursts of action. The aliens may find the game to be slow, boring, sometimes incomprehensible, and harder to appreciate than other sports.

But the appreciation, once attained, goes deeper. Baseball is like chess. Most of the action occurs in the head.

ROBERT THOM

The Gashouse Gang

Playing the Game

Pick-off moves

Leo Durocher

Yogi Berra

"Watching Frank Howard (left) come out of the Dodger dugout . . . is like watching the opening scene of a horror movie . . . the Earth rumbles and opens up, and out of it comes this Thing."

—Sportswriter
Jim Murray

SHORT PEOPLE *have one advantage in baseball—their strike zone is smaller. At 5 feet 11 inches, Pete Rose (below) would scrunch down in hopes of getting better pitches. Eddie Gaedel (above) didn't have to. The 3-feet-6-inch midget had a one-and-a-half-inch strike zone. In his one historic at bat for the St. Louis Browns in 1951, Gaedel walked on four pitches.*

The **Strike** *Zone*

Seventeen inches is the width of home plate and, according to the rules, the strike zone. Widen the zone one inch on each side and the defense gains an enormous advantage. Shrink it an inch and the offense feasts. Umpires are only human, and each has his own strike zone which may differ from other umpires either from side to side or up and down. Computers could be developed to read the strike zone and call every pitch perfectly. They would also rob the game of its soul.

WHERE WAS THAT PITCH? *The umpire sets up right over the catcher's shoulder, closest to the hitter. Some get so close to the catcher that they rest a hand on his back. Up until the 1980s, some umpires (below) still wore bulky foam "balloon" chest protectors outside their clothes. This forced them to position themselves above the catcher, and to call a slightly higher strike zone.*

Tinkering with the
Strike Zone

Baseball has been reluctant to tamper with the width of home plate, but the height of the strike zone has been changed regularly to maintain the delicate balance between offense and defense. When the rulemakers determine pitchers are too dominant, the strike zone is shrunk. When hitters regain control, the zone is expanded.

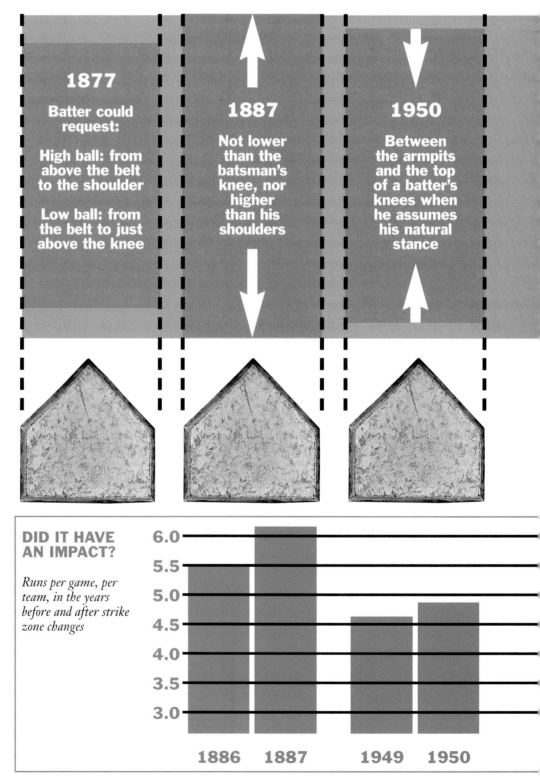

1877

Batter could request:

High ball: from above the belt to the shoulder

Low ball: from the belt to just above the knee

1887

Not lower than the batsman's knee, nor higher than his shoulders

1950

Between the armpits and the top of a batter's knees when he assumes his natural stance

DID IT HAVE AN IMPACT?

Runs per game, per team, in the years before and after strike zone changes

6.0
5.5
5.0
4.5
4.0
3.5
3.0

1886 1887   1949 1950

WHIZ KID *Philadelphia Phillie outfielder Del Ennis was a fine player for a dozen years in the majors; his career highs in the Triple Crown categories—homers, runs batted in, and batting average—came in 1950, perhaps as a result of the new, smaller strike zone.*

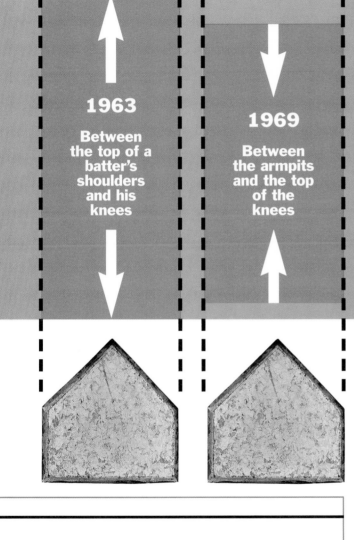

1963
Between the top of a batter's shoulders and his knees

1969
Between the armpits and the top of the knees

UPS AND DOWNS *Before 1887, hitters could instruct the pitcher to throw a pitch high or low. When that practice was discontinued, runs per game actually shot up. Maybe it was because batters were allowed four strikes in 1887. When the strike zone was made smaller in 1950, runs per game predictably went up. They went down when the strike zone was enlarged in 1963, and up again when it was squeezed tighter in 1969 (the same year the pitcher's mound was lowered).*

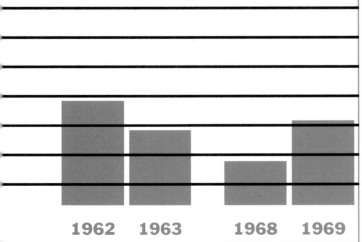

1962   1963   1968   1969

USING THE PLATE *Oakland's Dave Stewart pitching inside and outside to keep the hitter (Wade Boggs of the Red Sox) off stride during the 1990 American League Championship Series. Boggs, who struck out an average of only 42 times a year throughout his career, would fan twice in this game.*

"Some pitches are not meant to get a batter out but to set up another pitch that will. For example, inside pitches keep intimidated batters from reaching for pitches on the outside corner, even if they have two strikes against them."

—Tim McCarver

Working the
Strike Zone

Pitching is like real estate. What matters most is location, location, location. Even a pitcher who can blow minor league batters away with an overwhelming fastball learns quickly that major league hitters can time anyone. Accordingly, he must change speeds and spot the ball inside, outside, up, down, and sometimes off the plate to be effective. This is psychological warfare at its best. A pitcher might "set up" a batter by staying outside for two at bats, and then busting him inside when the game is on the line. The idea is to keep the hitter guessing, so he can't swing aggressively. Savvy pitchers and catchers use the strike zone the way artists use a canvas. But in baseball, the best ones only paint the corners.

FIGHTING FOR THE PLATE *Batters lean over the plate to reach the outside corner. Pitchers want to use the inside corner. Something's got to give. Usually, it's the batter's kneecap, ribs, or head. Don Drysdale (above) makes Vada Pinson eat dirt. "You've got to keep the ball away from the sweet part of the bat," claimed Drysdale. "To do that the pitcher has to move the hitter off the plate." Drysdale hit 143 batters in his career, a record.*

TED WILLIAMS'S STRIKE ZONE *This exhibit at the Baseball Hall of Fame represents how Williams felt he could hit pitches according to location. The Splendid Splinter liked the ball up, and felt he could only hit .230 on low, outside pitches. With a pitch down the middle, he considered himself a .400 hitter. For one whole season, he was. Williams hit .406 in 1941, the last time a player has cracked the .400 mark.*

PRECISION *Satchel Paige (left) had such good control that he would sometimes use a matchbook for his strike zone. "Just take the ball and throw it where you want to," he advised. "Home plate don't move."*

300	320	320	330	330	315	310
310	340	340	350	340	340	320
310	340	340	350	340	340	320
340	380	380	400	390	390	320
360	390	390	400	390	390	320
360	390	390	400	380	380	310
320	340	340	330	300	300	280
320	340	340		275	270	260
280	300	300	300	260	250	250
270	290	300	300	250	240	240
250			280	240	240	230

THE COUNT WAS 2-2 *when Babe Ruth hit perhaps his most famous homer in Game 3 of the 1932 World Series. Even if Ruth didn't actually "call his shot," it was audacious to be swinging for the fences with two strikes against him. Most hitters would concede the long ball in this situation and just try to put the ball in play.*

Getting ahead in The Count

With four balls and three strikes there are 11 possible counts, and each one conveys a FEELING. A hitter with an 0-2 count is grim-faced, a desperate man with his back is against a wall. At 1-2, he's still in bad shape, but with a fighting chance to survive. At 2-2 the count is even, but the pitcher still has breathing room while the batter does not.

With a 2-0 count, the batter is relaxed, confident, in control, a 2-1 count doesn't faze him much, and 3-1 feels like winning the lottery. The pitcher must hit the strike zone on the next pitch, probably with a fastball. All is well in the world.

With every strike, the advantage shifts slightly to the pitcher. With every ball, it moves toward the hitter. And when the count goes full at 3-2, it's the fans who have the advantage.

THE INDICATOR *is what the umpire uses to keep track of balls and strikes.*

"FOR IT'S ONE...TWO..THREE *strikes you're out at the old ballgame." Jack Norworth was on the New York City subway in 1908 when he saw a billboard advertising a New York Giants game. Norworth had never been to a baseball game, but he started scribbling lyrics on a scrap of paper and, by the time he got to his stop, baseball's anthem was finished. The song might have come out differently had Norworth written it a few decades earlier. In 1887, hitters were given four strikes. The number of balls allowed dropped from nine in 1876 to five in 1887 and finally to four in 1889.*

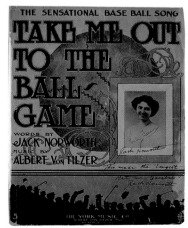

WADE BOGGS *is probably the best hitter with two strikes on him. He has a great eye for the strike zone and waits on the pitch before taking it or slapping it to the opposite field. That's also why he walks twice as often as he strikes out. In addition to his five batting titles, Boggs has led the American League six times in on base percentage.*

CHOKING UP *When behind in the count, some hitters, such as Wee Willie Keeler (above), grip the bat higher on the handle. This shortens the axis of rotation so they can move the bat more quickly to get a piece of the ball. But the shorter radius of swing means they will not hit the ball as far and will have a harder time reaching pitches on the outside corner.*

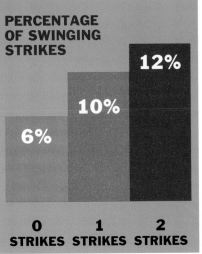

PERCENTAGE OF SWINGING STRIKES

6%	10%	12%
0 STRIKES	**1 STRIKES**	**2 STRIKES**

BLOWING IT BY 'EM *Batters were almost twice as likely to swing and miss at a two-strike offering than when they had no strikes.*

WAITING ON THE PITCH *Most batters like to give themselves as many pitches as possible, so they can get a good look at the pitcher's delivery.*

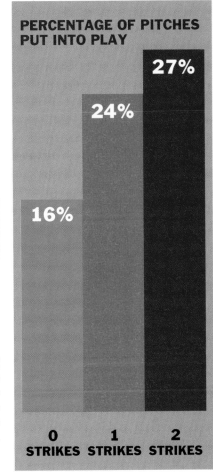

PERCENTAGE OF PITCHES PUT INTO PLAY

16%	24%	27%
0 STRIKES	**1 STRIKES**	**2 STRIKES**

WHAT HAPPENS WHEN?

Pitch counts at which the following events are ■ MOST LIKELY and ■ LEAST LIKELY to occur

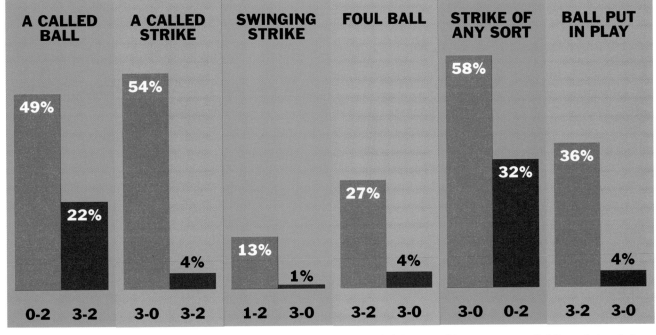

A CALLED BALL		A CALLED STRIKE		SWINGING STRIKE		FOUL BALL		STRIKE OF ANY SORT		BALL PUT IN PLAY	
49%	22%	54%	4%	13%	1%	27%	4%	58%	32%	36%	4%
0-2	**3-2**	**3-0**	**3-2**	**1-2**	**3-0**	**3-2**	**3-0**	**3-0**	**0-2**	**3-2**	**3-0**

STATS, INC. *keeps tabs on every pitch thrown in major league baseball; the charts on this page are compiled from their tabulations of the 583,496 pitches thrown during the 1992 season. What's the rarest of all events? A swing and a miss on a 3-0 pitch. That happened only 91 times in all of 1992.*

Rooting in the K Korner

The strikeout is not the most efficient way to get a batter out, but it is often the most rewarding for the pitcher. The pitcher gets more than an out. He gets a psychological advantage that lasts until the next time that batter puts the ball in play against him.

"Three strikes and you're out" makes intuitive sense, both in the batter's box and in society. If you make a mistake once, it could have been a fluke and you deserve another chance. If you make the mistake again, it appears that a pattern is setting in. And if you make it a third time, you have failed. Go sit down and let somebody else have a chance.

MOST STRIKEOUTS PER 9 INNINGS, CAREER

Randy Johnson	10.01
Nolan Ryan	9.57
Sandy Koufax	9.28
Lee Smith	8.87
Sam McDowell	8.86
J. R. Richard	8.37
Sid Fernandez	8.32
Eric Plunk	8.30
Roger Clemens	8.28
David Cone	8.15

Minimum 750 innings pitched

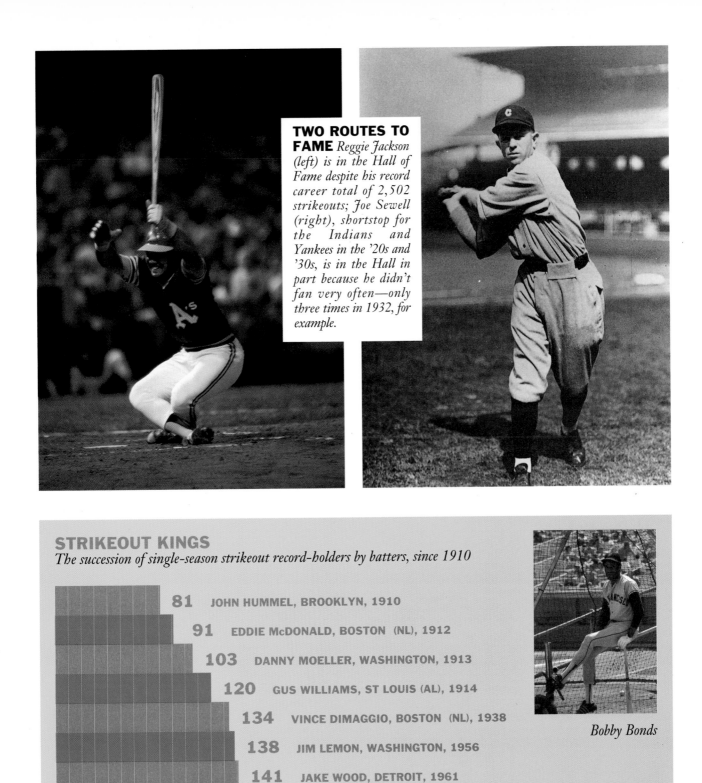

TWO ROUTES TO FAME *Reggie Jackson (left) is in the Hall of Fame despite his record career total of 2,502 strikeouts; Joe Sewell (right), shortstop for the Indians and Yankees in the '20s and '30s, is in the Hall in part because he didn't fan very often—only three times in 1932, for example.*

STRIKEOUT KINGS
The succession of single-season strikeout record-holders by batters, since 1910

81   JOHN HUMMEL, BROOKLYN, 1910

91   EDDIE McDONALD, BOSTON (NL), 1912

103   DANNY MOELLER, WASHINGTON, 1913

120   GUS WILLIAMS, ST LOUIS (AL), 1914

134   VINCE DIMAGGIO, BOSTON (NL), 1938

138   JIM LEMON, WASHINGTON, 1956

141   JAKE WOOD, DETROIT, 1961

142   HARMON KILLEBREW, MINNESOTA, 1962

175   DAVE NICHOLSON, CHICAGO (AL), 1963

187   BOBBY BONDS, SAN FRANCISCO, 1969

189   BOBBY BONDS, SAN FRANCISCO, 1970

Bobby Bonds

ELECTRIFYING *Bobby Bonds was a standout player for many years, but Bobby still holds the all-time record for whiffs in a season, a quarter century after setting the mark.*

STEVE BLASS DISEASE *As one of the NL's best control pitchers, Blass was 19-8 with a 2.49 ERA for the Pirates in 1972. The next season, he mysteriously couldn't find the plate. Blass tried meditation, therapy, hypnosis, and other cures, but within two years he was out of baseball.*

WALK THIS WAY *With 1,469 home runs between them, it's no wonder that sluggers like Babe Ruth (below, left) and Hank Aaron (below, right) got a total of 3,458 free passes to first base. But Eddie Yost (below, center) of the Washington Senators simply had a good eye for the strike zone. Yost walked over 100 times in eight seasons and led the American League in that category six times. He received so many bases on balls that his nickname was "The Walking Man."*

Oh, those
Bases on Balls

There are lots of reasons why a pitcher might purposely walk a batter. Maybe the hitter is a home-run threat and you'd rather issue a base on balls than let him hit a round tripper. Maybe first base is open and you want to put him on base to set up a double play. Maybe you think the next batter will be an easier out, so you don't give this one anything good to hit and see if he goes fishing for bad pitches.

Then, of course, there's the unintentional reason—you simply can't get the ball into the strike zone. A large percentage of hitters who walk eventually score. That's why the base on balls is a manager's nightmare. Legend has it that on his deathbed, Boston Braves manager George Stallings was asked what had caused his bad heart. Stallings groaned, "Oh, those bases on balls!" Then he closed his eyes and slipped away.

WALKS PER GAME, BY DECADE

1870s
1880s
1890s
1900s
1910s
1920s
1930s
1940s
1950s
1960s
1970s
1980s
1990s

1   2   3   4

NOLAN RYAN *struck out 5,714 batters, but he also walked 2,795. Ryan had virtually no control when he first came to the big leagues in 1966 and walked almost five batters per nine innings until he found the groove in his 14th season. In Ryan's case, a little wildness worked to his advantage. Hitters wouldn't get too comfy in the batter's box knowing the next pitch might be coming straight at them at 100 mph.*

A WALK IN THE PARK *Pitchers probably long for the good old days of the 1870s , when it took nine balls to walk a batter. In the 20th century walks per game increased along with home runs until pitchers regained dominance in the 1960s.*

Out of Control

Pressure has a nasty habit of robbing pitchers of their control. On several occasions, this has led to disaster. In 1904, Jack Chesbro of the New York Highlanders (who became the Yankees) had a career year. He had 30 complete games, 454 innings pitched, and an astonishing 41 wins. What fans remember, however, was how Chesbro blew the pennant on the last day of the season. It was the ninth inning, the game was tied at 2-2 and there was a runner at third when Chesbro threw a spitter (legal at the time) that sailed over his catcher's head.

Bob Moose of the Pittsburgh Pirates pitched a no-hitter in 1969. But Moose is remembered most for the time he bounced a wild pitch with two outs in the bottom of the ninth in Game 5 of the 1972 League Championship Series. George Foster scored from third and the Cincinnati Reds clinched the pennant.

Jack Chesbro, top, and Bob Moose

How to make enemies and intimidate people:

Head Games

Good hitting, pitching, and fielding are integral to winning a ballgame, of course. However, there are many perfectly legal things players and managers of all skill levels can do to mess with their opponent's mind and hopefully gain an edge.

BUST CHOPS *You can bet Chuck Tanner will lose the argument, but because he's putting up the fight, he hopes that next time the close call might go his way.*

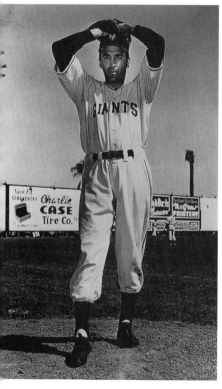

STICK IT IN HIS EAR
Sal Maglie was called "The Barber" because he enjoyed shaving chins with his fastball. "The second one lets the hitter know what you meant by the first one," he said.

GUILT BY ASSOCIATION
Managers will check a bat for cork to shake up an opposing hitter, make him look guilty, or simply to get a hot bat out of the game. Howard Johnson (left) frequently had his bat confiscated after his home-run production escalated in the late 1980s.

WE GOT ALL DAY *Baseball is known as a timeless game with no clock. Mike Hargrove used to take so much time getting set in the batter's box that he was known as "The Human Rain Delay."*

Gaylord Perry

"Before throwing his final 100 mph warm-up pitch high onto the backstop, Yankees reliever Ryne Duren would frighten batters not only with wildness but by wearing dark glasses—back then we didn't know he was both legally blind and an alcoholic. Gaylord Perry and Lew Burdette were the masters of head games, making batters think they were throwing spitters even if they weren't."

—**Tim McCarver**

CHOKE *The baseball commissioner fined pitcher Ryne Duren (above, right) $250 for giving the "choke" sign to an umpire during the 1958 World Series.*

RULES ARE RULES *Yankee's manager Billy Martin noticed that George Brett had too much pine tar on his bat, but he waited until Brett hit a big home run to tell the umpires. Brett went berserk when they took his homer away in this crucial 1983 game. The umpire was later overruled by the American League president.*

YA' BUM *"A baseball jockey,"* according to a 1941 Saturday Evening Post *article, "is a fellow who yells coarse, crude remarks at the gents of the opposition for the express purpose of covering them with confusion and frustration."* Fred Stanley of the Yankees (above) demonstrates.

SCARE 'EM SILLY *Ty Cobb, the story goes, would sit at the edge of the dugout and file his spikes razor sharp to scare the wits out of his opponent. In his later years he denied it. But what mattered was that opponents* thought *it was true.*

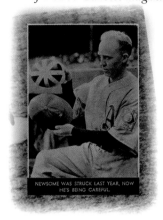

JOE "DUCKY" MEDWICK (*right*), *lies unconscious after getting beaned by ex-teammate Bob Bowman of the Cardinals in June 1940. Medwick recovered and hit .318 the next year to lead the Dodgers to their first pennant in two decades. Lamar Newsome of the Philadelphia Athletics (below) shows the protective helmet liner he used after a beaning, in this photo from a 1941 issue of* Police Gazette *magazine.*

NEWSOME WAS STRUCK LAST YEAR, NOW HE'S BEING CAREFUL.

DEATH IN THE AFTERNOON *Ray Chapman (above, left) was the only man killed by a pitched ball in major league history. The popular Cleveland shortstop was beaned by submariner Carl Mays of the Yankees (above, right) on August 16, 1920, at the Polo Grounds. The Indians went on to win the World Series in Chapman's honor. Mays went on to a very successful career (207-126, 2.92 ERA).*

And now for a little chin music

Beanballs

The pitcher's biggest weapon is often not his fastball, curve, or change-up. It's intimidation. A swiftly thrown baseball can kill a man—and has. The remote possibility of getting hit by a pitched ball is what keeps many hitters from digging in at the plate. Pitchers learn early that they must back hitters off the plate, and, on rare occasions, feel it necessary to plunk one to send a message—"Move back, I own the plate," or sometimes "Your teammate took me over the wall, so you're going down."

Despite all efforts to prevent them, beanballs—or the threat of beanballs—remain an integral part of the game. They're like nuclear weapons: their mere existence, in nearly all cases, makes it unnecessary to use them.

TONY C *Tony Conigliaro hit 32 home runs for his hometown Red Sox in 1965 as a 20-year-old. After his cheekbone was broken by a Jack Hamilton fastball on August 18, 1967, his vision was so poor he missed the entire 1968 season. Tony C came back in 1969 and smashed 36 homers in 1970, but recurring eye problems caused his early retirement in 1971.*

"When I play the outfield or infield, it's almost like not playing at all. Catching is the most important job in baseball."

—Johnny Bench

The catcher as
Field General

He is the only player who positions himself in foul territory. He has to in order to watch the entire field. The catcher is a baseball team's field general. In addition to the ability to call pitches, block the plate, and throw out base stealers, there are further qualifications for the job. The catcher must be a leader of men who commands respect from his teammates. He needs good communication skills. He's got to be a psychologist. He must know the strengths and weaknesses of his pitchers and those of every hitter in the league. He needs a quick, alert, decisive mind. He needs to be a master strategist. Finally, he must be the heart, soul, and inspiration of his team. With these qualities, it's not surprising that many catchers have gone on to become major league managers. To name a few: Yogi Berra, Connie Mack, Mickey Cochrane, Gabby Hartnett, Ralph Houk, Al Lopez, Wilbert Robinson, Birdie Tebbetts, Joe Torre.

THURMAN MUNSON *played less than a hundred games in the minors, but had an intuitive grasp for handling veteran pitchers and being a team leader. Munson was the American League Rookie of the Year in 1970, Most Valuable Player in 1976, and he led the Yankees to back-to-back World Championships in 1977 and 1978.*

YOGI BERRA *"observed a lot by watching."*

FREE COUNSELING *Tim McCarver is one of the few players whose career spanned four decades (including eight games in 1959 and six in 1980). McCarver and Steve "Lefty" Carlton (opposite) had a celebrated argument over pitch selection when Carlton was a rookie with the Cardinals in 1965. The pair eventually got on the same wavelength and when Carlton was traded to the Phillies, he requested they get McCarver too. Tim became Steve's "personal catcher." McCarver says that when they die, they'll be buried sixty feet and six inches apart.*

Keeping 'em **Close**

A fast runner can make it from first base to second base in about 3.5 seconds. It takes a pitcher about 1.3 seconds to wind up, and about .6 for his pitch to reach the plate. That leaves just 1.6 for the catcher to catch the ball, make an accurate peg to second, and for the tag to be applied. There's no margin for error. If the base runner has a good jump, it's almost impossible for even the best catcher to throw him out. For that reason, pitchers must work hard to keep runners close to the bag, and to deliver their pitches quickly.

PICKOFF PLAY *Maury Wills didn't get picked off much, but pitcher Al Jackson of the Mets (above) nails him and Ed Kranepool applies the tag. Runners will get picked off if they take too big a lead, become fooled by the pitcher's delivery, or if they simply are caught "napping."*

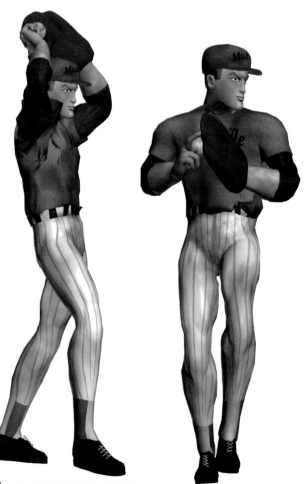

WINDUP OR STRETCH *A windup with a leg kick (near right) gives the pitcher leverage to throw as hard as he can. That's fine when the bases are empty. But it takes up valuable milliseconds. With runners on base, pitchers dispense with the kick and pitch from the "set" or "stretch" position (far right) where they simply stride forward and deliver the pitch.*

HOLDING 'EM ON *Left-handers have an easier time than righties do in holding runners on—they're staring at first base as they wind up. Terry Mulholland (above left) was so good at holding runners on that few even tried to steal on him. Mulholland didn't allow a single stolen base in 1994 and just one in 1993. Rick Aguilera (above right) ordinarily has a good move to first. However, from 1993 through 1995 runners stole 24 consecutive bases on him.*

THROWING OVER *Some pitchers throw over to first endlessly to hold runners close. Others rarely throw over. Stats Inc. research shows that stolen-base percentage does seem to drop slightly when a pitcher throws over repeatedly. Diving back to first uses up a runner's energy, and perhaps slows him down when he finally does attempt the steal. Rickey Henderson (right) tormenting an unfortunate pitcher.*

"A catcher might call for the pickoff if the runner seems to be leaning toward the next base. Or when the runner seems so distracted by the intense pitcher-batter confrontation or by the catcher using his fingers to indicate what and where the next pitch will be that he forgets he's not standing safely on the bag. When the runner least expects it—that's when the catcher wants to call for a pitchout!"

—Tim McCarver

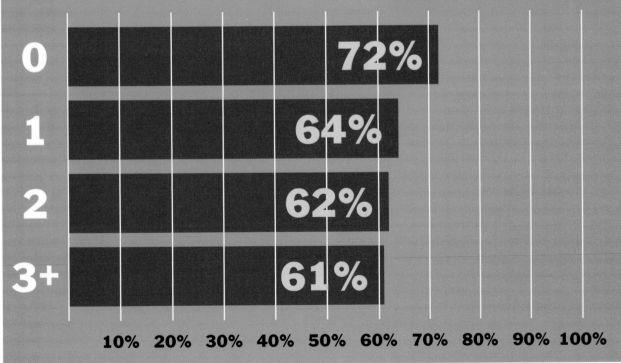

STOLEN BASE PERCENTAGE BY NUMBER OF PICKOFF THROWS

PICKOFF THROWS

0	72%
1	64%
2	62%
3+	61%

10% 20% 30% 40% 50% 60% 70% 80% 90% 100%

The art of the **Steal**

THE KEY *to stealing bases is to study the pitcher's motion in order to know the instant he has committed to throwing the pitch. A great base stealer like Rickey Henderson (above) will pick up a telltale sign from the pitcher's heel, shoulder, knee, head, or elbow. After breaking for second, it's crucial for the runner to glance toward home plate to determine the batter's status. If the ball has been popped up, he'll have to scoot back to first. If it has been hit on the ground, he might have to break up a double play. If it has gone through the infield for a hit, he'll round second and keep going.*

The stolen base is a fascinating game of cat-and-mouse. As soon as a runner reaches first base, the wheels begin to turn in the players minds: Is he a threat to steal? Is the pitcher good at holding runners on? Will he throw the pitch or throw over to first? Can the runner get a good lead? A good jump? Will the manager give him the green light? On which pitch? How's the catcher's arm? Can the hitter "protect" the runner? Who's going to cover second base? How will the game situation be changed if the runner is on second? What if he gets thrown out? This is one of those baseball situations in which the players seem to be standing around, but the real game is being played inside their heads.

"When you steal a base, 99 percent of the time you steal on a pitcher. You actually never steal on a catcher. In order to be a good base stealer, you must study the mechanics of a pitcher's style—how he delivers it to the hitter."

—Lou Brock

"It's just as important to know when not to go as it is to know when to go."

—Maury Wills

RACING THE PITCH *to the plate is thrilling, but stealing home is a low percentage play that is rarely seen anymore. Jackie Robinson (above) pulled it off 19 times, including once in the World Series. Robinson was a terror on the basepaths and murder in a rundown, but he played in an era when stolen bases were very rare. In his rookie season, he led the National League with only 29 steals. Two years later he led the League again with 37. He only stole 197 bases in his career compared to 18 players who have stolen 600 in their careers.*

GERMANY SCHAEFER *of the Tigers is the only player to steal first base, in 1908. He was on first and teammate Davy Jones was on third. Schaefer broke for second base hoping the catcher's throw would enable Jones to score, but the catcher didn't throw. Standing on second base, Schaefer yelled to Jones, "Let's try it again."* On the next pitch, he ran back and stole FIRST. The catcher was so rattled that when Schaefer broke for second again, he threw the ball away and Jones scored. After this incident, a new rule was adopted: "Any runner is out when, after he has acquired legal possession of a base, he runs the bases in reverse order for the purpose of confusing the defense or making a travesty of the game."*

SLIDING BILLY HAMILTON *of the Phillies was the first great base stealer, known for his headfirst slides. He led the National League in steals seven times, swiped seven bases in one 1894 game, and stole 117 in 1889 (in those days, stolen bases were credited when baserunners advanced more bases than the batter got with a hit).*

Charting the **Steal**

Stealing bases was a big part of the game before Babe Ruth and the other sluggers of the 1920s came along. Why would anybody risk stealing when the guy at the plate might very well put the next pitch over the fence? Stealing bases virtually disappeared from the game by 1950, when Dom DiMaggio led the American League with just 15 steals. The stolen base made a comeback in the 1960s, thanks to the emergence of exciting players, artificial turf, and a more aggressive style of play.

MAURY WILLS *sliding into one of the 104 bases he stole in 1962 to break Ty Cobb's record of 96. It is Wills who is usually credited with bringing the stolen base back to baseball.*

STOLEN BASES PER GAME (BOTH TEAMS), BY DECADE

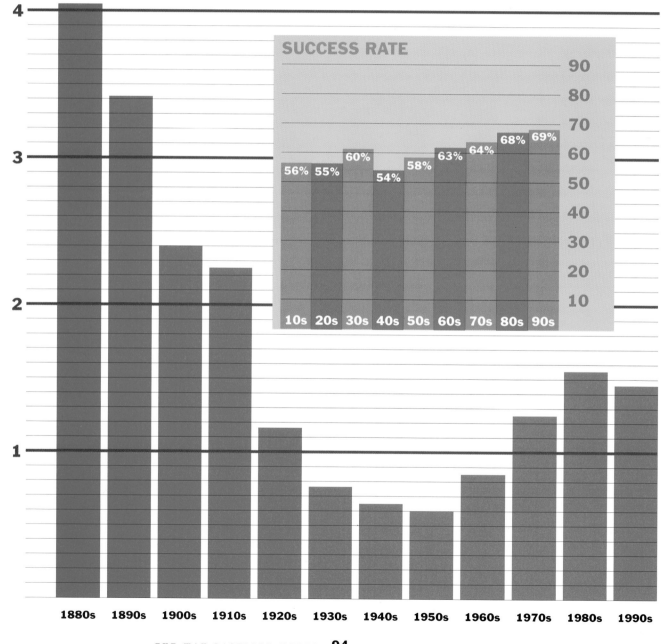

SUCCESS RATE

10s	20s	30s	40s	50s	60s	70s	80s	90s
56%	55%	60%	54%	58%	63%	64%	68%	69%

1880s 1890s 1900s 1910s 1920s 1930s 1940s 1950s 1960s 1970s 1980s 1990s

Left to right: Ken Williams, Willie Mays, Bobby Bonds

Power & speed: The 30/30 Club

Most power hitters don't run well. Most speedsters don't hit with power. Few players have the combination of power and speed necessary to hit 30 home runs and steal 30 bases in the same season. Most of the members of the 30/30 club, as can be seen here, joined since the 1970s, the first era in which stolen bases and home runs were used as potent offensive weapons at the same time.

THE 30/30 CLUB		HR	SB
1922	Ken Williams, St.L (AL)	39	37
1956	Willie Mays, NY (NL)	36	40
1957	Willie Mays, NY (NL)	35	38
1963	Hank Aaron, Mil	44	31
1969	Bobby Bonds, SF	32	45
1970	Tommy Harper, Mil	31	38
1973	Bobby Bonds, SF	39	43
1975	Bobby Bonds, NY (AL)	32	30
1977	Bobby Bonds, Cal	37	41
1983	Dale Murphy, Atl	36	30
1987	Howard Johnson, NY (NL)	36	32
1987	Joe Carter, Cle	32	31
1987	Darryl Strawberry, NY (NL)	39	36
1987	Eric Davis, Cin	37	50
1988	Jose Canseco, Oak	42	40
1989	Howard Johnson, NY (NL)	36	41
1990	Barry Bonds, Pit	33	52
1990	Ron Gant, Atl	32	33
1991	Howard Johnson, NY (NL)	38	30
1991	Ron Gant, Atl	32	34
1992	Barry Bonds, Pit	34	39
1993	Sammy Sosa, Chi (NL)	33	36
1995	Sammy Sosa, Chi (NL)	36	34
1995	Barry Bonds, SF	33	31

JOSE CANSECO *is the first—and only—member of the 40/40 club. In 1988 he slammed 42 homers and stole 40 bases. He walks off the field (above) with number 40.*

SLIDE, KELLY, SLIDE! *Mike King Kelly, hero of the Chicago White Stockings in the 1880s, popularized the hook slide. Kelly swiped 84 bases in 1887, and was so famous in his time that he became the subject of a hit song: "Your running's a disgrace/Stay there, hold your base!/If someone doesn't steal you/and your batting doesn't fail you/they'll take you to Australia!/Slide, Kelly, Slide!" Kelly's final words, while falling off a stretcher after catching pneumonia, were, "This is my last slide."*

FIGURE-4 SLIDE *or "bent leg slide" is the simplest and safest slide. The runner tucks one leg under the other to form a number 4 shape. His hands should be back out of harm's way, his head up watching the base, which he touches with his straight leg. The Figure-4 can be turned into a "pop-up" slide, in which the runner uses the base as a brace and pops immediately to a standing position so he can advance to the next base.*

THE RECORD *Rickey Henderson stealing his 939th base in 1991, which broke the lifetime mark set by Lou Brock (which broke Ty Cobb's record of 892).*

HEADFIRST SLIDES *have become popular, thanks to aggressive runners like Pete Rose (above) and Rickey Henderson. The runner dives horizontal and low, with his palms down and fingers up. The hands touch the ground and the base first. Headfirst slides get you there faster, and are safer now that helmets and batting gloves have become standard equipment. But even with protection, very few players attempt to slide into home headfirst, where a well-protected catcher is likely to be waiting.*

Sliding

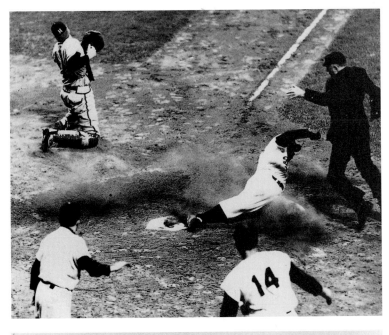

The ball and runner are streaking toward third base from different directions and will arrive at virtually the same instant. The third baseman braces himself for the collision and concentrates intensely on catching the ball and slapping down his glove. The runner leaves his feet and swoops down into the dirt to evade the tag, knock the ball loose, or simply kick up a swirl of dust to obscure the umpire's view. The slide can be baseball's most exciting moment.

THE HOOK SLIDE *is used if the runner needs to elude a tag on a throw that has beaten him to the base. The runner rolls his upper body out of the way and hooks the bag with a toe, leaving very little to tag. This is demonstrated by Jackie Robinson (top left) and Ty Cobb (left).*

TAKEOUT SLIDE *When forced out at second, the runner at first is instructed to upend the second baseman or shortstop in order to ruin ("break up") the double play. Usually, he will aim for the infielder's left foot to disrupt the throw. At right, Billy Martin takes out Ray Boone in a 1953 game between the Yankees and Indians.*

"'Bad' baserunners aren't necessarily the players who are thrown out trying for an extra base but the ones who are too timid to take such chances on balls hit to the outfield or pitches that bounce in the dirt."

—Tim McCarver

Running the
Bases

How many times have you heard an announcer say, "He's not fast, but he's an excellent base runner"? Running the bases requires instinct, common sense, intelligence, courage, and aggressiveness. From the Chicago White Sox's Hitless Wonders (1900s) to St. Louis's Gashouse Gang (1930s) to the Go-Go Sox (1950s) to Oakland A's Billyball (1980s), teams have won ballgames without using their bats, balls, or gloves. They're won on the basepaths.

ROUNDING THIRD *Like a bicycle racer, Ty Cobb tilts his body at an angle to round the corner more quickly. He is using the front, inside corner of the bag as a brace to push off and aggressively drive his body toward home in this classic photo.*

THE GASHOUSE GANG *In this painting by Robert Thom, Pepper Martin of the St. Louis Cardinals crashes into third. The Cardinals (with Pepper Martin, Leo Durocher, Frankie Frisch, Ducky Medwick, and Dizzy and Daffy Dean) were known for aggressive play. Sportswriters dubbed Martin "The Wild Horse of the Osage."*

THE ELEMENT OF SURPRISE *In Game 7 of the 1946 World Series, Enos "Country" Slaughter of the Cardinals (right) had the nerve to dash from first base all the way home on a routine single by Harry Walker. Slaughter scored the winning run and the Boston Red Sox were denied the championship.*

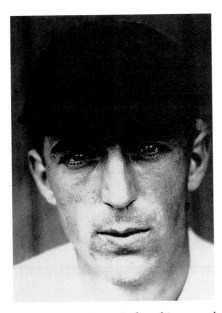

BONEHEAD *Instead of touching second when his teammate drove in the game-winning run to end a 1908 game, New York Giant Fred Merkle (above) left the field. Johnny Evers of the Cubs got the ball, forced Merkle out, and nullified the run. The Cubs went on to win the pennant by a game, and Merkle was nicknamed "bonehead" for the rest of his life.*

SPEED LIMITS *Oakland owner Charlie Finley hired track star Herb Washington, assuming the fastest man in the world would be able to steal lots of bases. Unfortunately, Washington had no baseball instincts. Here he is (above) getting picked off first in the ninth inning of Game 2 of the 1974 World Series. He represented the tying run.*

GET IN THE WAY *Base runners know that if they get hit by a thrown ball, there is little chance the fielder will catch it. J. C. Martin (left) of the Mets was the star in this controversial play in the tenth inning of Game 4 of the 1969 World Series. With a runner on second, Martin bunted toward pitcher Pete Richert, then ran to first base on the infield side of the foul line. Richert's throw hit him on the wrist, and the game-winning run scored. Oriole manager Earl Weaver claimed Martin ran inside the line, but the umps didn't*

The art of the Sacrifice Bunt

In no other sport does an athlete specifically attempt to fail (make an out) and give up his chance to be the hero for the greater good of his team. Getting runners into scoring position (second or third base) is how ballgames are won, and the sacrifice bunt is often the best way to do it.

LEGEND *has it that Dickie Pearce of the Brooklyn Atlantics introduced the bunt in 1856.*

As the pitcher winds up, the batter suddenly pivots ("squares around") on his back foot to face the mound. He slides his top hand halfway up the bat, his lower hand stays a few inches up from the knob. He holds the bat level, high in the strike zone, and with a relaxed grip. He "catches" the ball with the bat to deaden it and angles the bat to send the ball down the first baseline (when there's a runner on first) or third baseline (when there are runners at first and second). A well-executed bunt is beautiful, and the batter who gives up his potential glory to advance the runner along will receive congratulations all around as he returns to the dugout.

NOT TOO HARD, NOT TOO SOFT *The idea of a bunt is to drop the ball in front of the infielders and far enough away from the catcher so the runner at first can advance to second base safely. Johnny Temple of the Reds (above) demonstrates. The infielders will make the easy out at first rather than risk a tough play at second, which, if it fails, could ignite a big inning of scoring.*

BRETT BUTLER *is one of the game's best bunters in recent years. Not only does he execute the sacrifice well, Butler has also had 20 or more bunt hits in ten consecutive seasons.*

GOOD BUNT *Hall of Famer Edd Roush shows how it's done.*

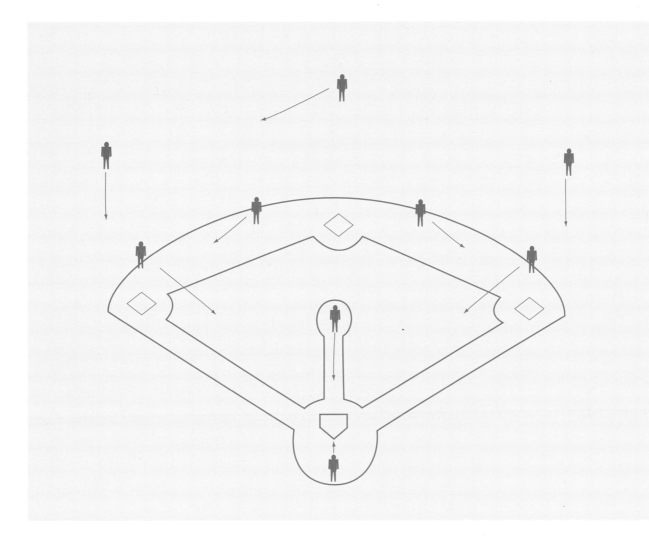

DEFENDING THE BUNT *In a typical bunting situation with a runner at first, the first baseman and third baseman charge toward home to field the ball. The shortstop covers second base, the second baseman covers first base, and the pitcher covers the area in front of the mound. In a situation with runners at first and second base, third base must be covered and the pitcher may have to pick up bunts down the third baseline. In a variation called "the wheel play," (above) the shortstop dashes to cover third, allowing the third baseman to charge for the bunt.*

BAD BUNT *If the batter taps the ball too far, the infielders can scoop it up and make the force play at second, if not a double play. That's what happened to Hank Bauer of the Yankees (right). Power hitters are notoriously poor bunters, and Casey Stengel probably wished he'd let Bauer swing away.*

UNIVERSAL TRUTHS *of the game
are revealed to Yankee manager
Casey Stengel and his coaches.*

Going by the Book

"I never play by the book," Dick Williams once boasted, "because I never met the guy that wrote it." Most players and managers, however, base decisions strictly on "the book"—a collection of unwritten rules that have been passed down through the generations. For instance: NEVER MAKE THE FIRST OUT AT HOME PLATE. This maxim makes sense because with two outs, the team has three chances to score a runner from third. It would be foolish for that runner to risk getting thrown out at the plate when there's such a good chance one of the next hitters will drive him in.

Managers learn to "play the percentages," even when they don't know what the percentages are. Those who violate the game's conventional wisdom are accused of the heinous sin of "going against the book."

Summer Reading

● **ON OFFENSE, IT IS BEST TO HAVE HIT-TERS FACE OPPOSITE-HANDED PITCHERS. ON DEFENSE, IT IS BEST TO HAVE PITCH-ERS FACE SAME-HANDED HITTERS.** *It's easi-er to hit a pitch that is coming toward you than a pitch moving away from you. A lefthander's pitch moves away from a lefthanded batter and toward a righthanded batter. It's the opposite for a right-handed pitcher.*

● **IF FIRST BASE IS OPEN AND RUNNERS ARE AT SECOND AND THIRD, WALK THE NUMBER EIGHT HITTER AND PITCH TO THE PITCHER INSTEAD.** *In this situation, a single scores two runs. Rather than give the number eight hitter a chance to hit one, put him on base and pitch to the pitcher, who is almost always the worst hitter in the lineup.*

● **NEVER WALK A BATTER WHO REPRE-SENTS THE TYING OR GO-AHEAD RUN.** *A significant percentage of batters who receive a base on balls eventually score. Losing a game is never fun, but it hurts even more when you gave the winning run a free pass to first base.*

● **NEVER TAKE THE BAT OUT OF THE HANDS OF YOUR BEST HITTER.** *If you've got*

"First and third, nobody out. You're talking about a big inning. To me, the secret of scoring a lot of runs is, as many times as you can get a guy into scoring position, do it."

—Tony LaRussa

runners on base and a guy at the plate who gets a hit every three times he comes to bat, don't try to steal a base. You want to give your hitter the chance to drive in the runs. If a runner is caught stealing for the third out, your best hitter will lead off the next inning with no baserunners to drive in.

● IF YOU'VE GOT AN 0-2 COUNT ON THE BATTER, PUT THE NEXT PITCH OUT OF THE STRIKE ZONE. *The pitcher has a big advantage in this situation. He has four balls to work with, while the hitter has his back against the wall and must protect the plate against strike three. If you throw a ball, the hitter might go fishing for it and strike out. And if he doesn't, you can try again. But if you throw a strike, he might hit it hard and you've wasted your advantage.*

● WHEN YOU'RE PLAYING AT HOME, PLAY FOR A TIE. WHEN YOU'RE ON THE ROAD, GO FOR THE WIN. *The home team bats in the bottom half of the inning, so they always have another chance to win the game. The important thing is to at least tie the game so they get the chance to score and win it in the next inning. The visiting team doesn't get "last licks," so they have to hope to get a lead and hold it.*

● IF THERE'S A RUNNER ON FIRST BASE, HIT THE BALL TO THE RIGHT SIDE OF THE FIELD. *Advancing runners to scoring position is crucial to scoring runs. A grounder to the right side, even if it doesn't go through the infield, will probably advance the runner to second. A grounder to the left side, on the other hand, will very possibly result in a double play.*

● IF THE TEAM IS BEHIND, HITTERS SHOULD TAKE A STRIKE. *When you're losing, you want to get runners on base any way you can to get a rally started. Waiting for the first strike may result in getting a few balls if the pitcher doesn't have good control. With luck the hitter will get a base on balls, or at least get ahead in the count.*

● IF YOU'VE GOT A RIGHTY PITCHING, DON'T

WALK A RIGHT-HANDED HITTER TO GET TO A LEFT-HANDED HITTER. *Even if the left-handed batter is weaker than the right-handed batter, you'd rather pitch to the righty because of the natural advantage your pitcher has against right-handed batters.*

● WITH AN 0-2 COUNT, DON'T TRY THE HIT-AND-RUN PLAY. *You put on the hit-and-run with a count where the pitcher is likely to put the pitch in the strike zone (3-1 or 2-1, for instance), so your hitter gets a good pitch to hit. On an 0-2 count, the pitcher will probably put the ball out of the strike zone, and if your hitter is forced to swing he will most likely strike out.*

● IF YOUR TEAM IS WAY AHEAD OR WAY BEHIND, DON'T ATTEMPT TO STEAL BASES OR TAKE AN EXTRA BASE. *When you're way behind, you play conservatively because a risk that fails will kill a potential rally that might have allowed you to catch up. When you're way ahead, you play conservatively so you don't humiliate your opponent.*

● IF THERE ARE TWO OUTS, DON'T ATTEMPT TO STEAL THIRD. *The risk isn't worth the reward. You're already in scoring position at second base. A single will probably score you from there. You won't be much better off at third with two outs, because you can't tag up on a fly ball. So why attempt a risky steal that will end the inning if you're thrown out?*

● DON'T BRING THE INFIELD IN UNTIL LATE IN THE GAME. *Bringing the infield in severely reduces the effectiveness of your defense. Balls shoot through and pop over drawn-in infields very easily. You only want to bring the infield in as a desperation move, when there are less than two outs and a runner at third who can tie or win the game. You've got to hope for a hard ground ball right at somebody, so you can throw the runner out at the plate. Early in the game, however, you should concede the run in this situation. That clears the bases and prevents a big inning. You'll have time to catch up later.*

SATCHELL PAIGE'S RULES FOR STAYING YOUNG:

1. Avoid fried meats which angry up the blood.

2. If your stomach disputes you, lie down and pacify it with cool thoughts.

3. Keep the juices flowing by jangling around gently as you move.

4. Go very lightly on the vices, such as carrying on in society—the social ramble ain't restful.

5. Avoid running at all times.

6. Don't look back. Something might be gaining on you.

THE WAY BASEBALL WORKS **103** PLAYING THE GAME

"The secret of managing a club is to keep the five guys who hate you away from the five guys who are undecided."
—Casey Stengel

The Manager

If the catcher is the field general, the manager is the commander in chief of the army. During a game he makes the strategic and tactical decisions—when to swing away, take a pitch, steal, bunt, pitch out, hit and run, bring in a reliever, send up a pinch hitter, bring the infield in, argue a call, and an infinite number of other details that may mean the difference between winning and losing a game. But the manager's job is much more than that. He also helps select his players, train them, teach them, discipline them, coddle them, and make them rise to the occasion when necessary.

After all that, the manager will be second-guessed on every decision he makes and eventually, when his team loses enough games, he will probably be fired. "There are only two kinds of managers," Gil Hodges once said. "Winning managers and ex-managers."

VIEWERS WERE TRANSFIXED *as Reggie Jackson and Billy Martin (top) just about had a fistfight in the Yankees dugout during this 1977 game in Boston after Reggie allegedly failed to hustle for a fly ball. Left, top to bottom, legendary managers John McGraw and Miller Huggins; Connie Mack's perch for 53 years; and Sparky Anderson—the only manager to win over 850 games and a world championship in each league.*

HANDS-ON *manager Leo Durocher (left) would sometimes run his team from the first base coach's box. Several of baseball's familiar signs were invented by William "Dummy" Hoy (1862-1961), a deaf player who was having trouble communicating with teammates and umpires.*

Filling out the Lineup

One of the manager's important jobs is to design a batting order that will get the most run production from the varying abilities of his players. Conventional wisdom says he should look for these qualities in the nine slots of his batting order:

LEADOFF *hitter extraordinaire Rickey Henderson*

CASEY STENGEL *(above) won 10 pennants in 12 years with the Yankees. "I couldn'tna done it without my players," he quipped. That's for sure. When Casey managed the Mets, he finished dead last all four years. Earl Weaver (right) guided the Orioles to first place five times in a six-year span.*

1. The leadoff hitter must get on base frequently, perhaps four times out of ten at bats. To do this, he needs a good eye for the strike zone, patience so he can draw walks, good bat control, and the speed to beat out infield grounders.

2. The second hitter should be a good contact hitter who can hit the ball to the right side on the hit-and-run play or simply to advance the runner. He should be able to bunt well. He must have speed to stay out of the double play. Left-handers are desirable because they stand in the way of a catcher's view of first base.

3. This is where the manager puts his best all-around hitter, a guy who has some power and can drive in runs. He should be fast enough to stay out of double plays, draw a decent number of walks, and not strike out too much.

IDEAL *number three hitter, Willie Mays*

4. The cleanup hitter should be the man with the highest slugging average, who can change the game with one swing of the bat.

5. The next best cleanup hitter goes here.

6. The number sixth hitter is sort of like a second leadoff man (especially if the previous guys cleared the bases).

7. The manager wants a guy here who can advance the runner, maybe pull off the hit and run.

8. & 9. Generally the weakest hitters go here. Frequently, they don't even get a time at bat until the third inning. In the National League, where there is no designated hitter, the pitcher bats ninth.

THOSE WHO CAN, TEACH *People said Ted Williams couldn't manage because he wouldn't be able to handle players less skilled than himself. But Williams was named Manager of the Year after his Washington Senators went 86-76 in 1969, a 21-game improvement over the previous year. Babe Ruth's biggest disappointment was never getting the chance to manage. He coached the Boston Braves briefly, but his job was mainly to attract fans to the ballpark.*

CALL TO THE BULLPEN
Cleveland manager Mike Hargrove lifts starter Dennis Martinez.

Managing a
Pitching Staff

Al Spalding and Greg Maddux were the best pitchers of their times. In 1875 Spalding started 72 games, won 55 of them, finished 52, and pitched 575 innings. In 1993 Maddux started 36 games, won 20 of them, finished 8, and pitched 267 innings. Over the decades managers have totally changed the way they handled their pitching staffs. The three-man rotation gave way to the four-man rotation, and today most teams use a five-man rotation. Pitchers get fewer starts, fewer innings pitched, fewer chances for a 20-win season, and some experts claim, fewer arm problems.

Managing a pitching staff is a delicate skill. Some pitchers require a lot of rest between starts, others feel rusty unless they get the ball every few days.

TOMORROW'S PITCHER *usually charts today's game, recording the results of each pitch for future reference.*

Knuckleballers use very little energy to throw their specialty, so they can pitch more frequently than power pitchers. Care must be taken to avoid blowing out the arm of an enthusiastic young pitcher. The manager shouldn't always think only in terms of who can win the game today, but how he can win at the end of the season and in the years to come.

BALTIMORE PITCHERS

Jim Palmer, Dave McNally, Pat Dobson, and Mike Cuellar all won 20 or more games in 1971. This was partly due to their skill and partly due to the managing of Earl Weaver, who had at least one 20-game winning pitcher for 13 straight seasons. Weaver's philosophy: the four-man rotation, mixing pitches, throwing breaking balls for strikes, and little emphasis on strikeouts.

THE DECLINE OF THE COMPLETE GAME

Percentage of games completed by starting pitchers, American League, 1901–1995

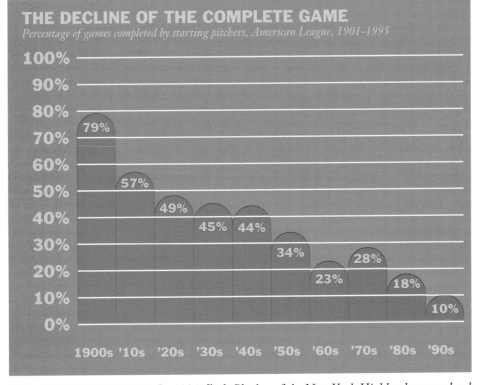

Decade	%
1900s	79%
'10s	57%
'20s	49%
'30s	45%
'40s	44%
'50s	34%
'60s	23%
'70s	28%
'80s	18%
'90s	10%

WORKHORSES *Stan Bahnsen (above, left) and Wilbur Wood (above, right) worked on two days rest for the White Sox in the early 1970s as an experiment by pitching coach Johnny Sain (below). Wood went from 9-13 to 22-13 in 1971, and also won 20 or more games the next three years. Bahnsen had his best year (21-16) in 1972.*

ENDANGERED SPECIES *In 1904, Jack Chesbro of the New York Highlanders completed 48 of the 51 games he started. In 1991 the entire New York Yankee staff had three complete games. The extinction of the complete game was temporarily postponed when the American League introduced the designated hitter in 1973. Managers did not have to take out their pitcher to use a pinch hitter in close games, so starters finished more games.*

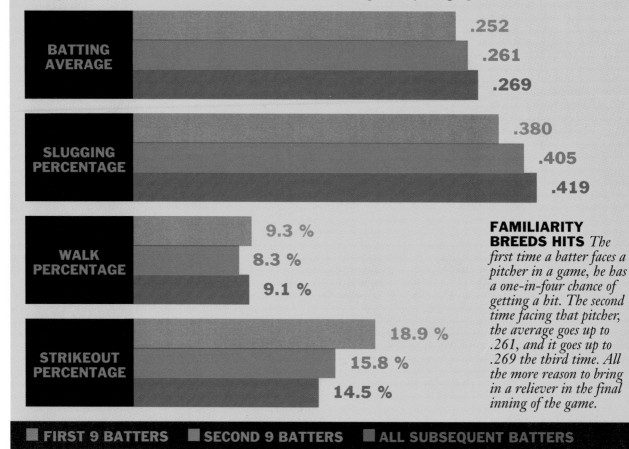

THRICE THROUGH THE BATTING ORDER

Batting records of the first nine, second nine, and subsequent batters against major league pitchers, 1986-1988

BATTING AVERAGE
.252
.261
.269

SLUGGING PERCENTAGE
.380
.405
.419

WALK PERCENTAGE
9.3 %
8.3 %
9.1 %

STRIKEOUT PERCENTAGE
18.9 %
15.8 %
14.5 %

FAMILIARITY BREEDS HITS *The first time a batter faces a pitcher in a game, he has a one-in-four chance of getting a hit. The second time facing that pitcher, the average goes up to .261, and it goes up to .269 the third time. All the more reason to bring in a reliever in the final inning of the game.*

■ **FIRST 9 BATTERS**   ■ **SECOND 9 BATTERS**   ■ **ALL SUBSEQUENT BATTERS**

Some 20th-century **Firemen**

CY YOUNG *won 30 games as a reliever. Top pitchers of the era like Christy Mathewson, Mordecai Brown, Grover Cleveland Alexander, Walter Johnson, and Lefty Grove all worked in relief regularly. Today, relievers are considered almost a different species from starters.*

JOE PAGE *struggled as a starting pitcher, but blossomed when he went to the Yankee bullpen in 1947. He had 14 relief wins that season and 13 in 1949, with 27 saves.*

1910   **1920**   **1930**   **1940**

ERNIE SHORE *made perhaps the most famous relief appearance on June 23, 1917. Babe Ruth started pitching the game for the Red Sox and was ejected after he walked the first hitter and argued with the umpire. The runner was caught stealing, and Shore retired the next 26 batters in a row, the equivalent of a perfect game.*

■ **FIRPO MARBERRY** *was one of the first pitchers to be used exclusively as a reliever. The "save" was officially recognized as a stat in 1969, but researchers have credited Marberry with 101 saves between 1924 and 1934, including a high of 22 in 1926..*

The rise of the **Relief Pitcher**

Once upon a time, people finished what they started. Pitchers didn't leave a game unless they were pounded. Relief pitchers were washed-up starters. There was this common statistic called "the complete game."

Today, it's the relievers who are the celebrities. Starters are routinely lifted in the eighth or ninth inning even though they're not tired or in trouble.

There are a number of reasons for this change, but the biggest reason is simple: it made sense. Sure, there's something to be said for the starter being out there on the mound to get the last out in the ninth and receive handshakes from his teammates. But it makes more sense strategically to have a pitcher work seven or eight strong innings, then bring in a rested arm or two to nail down the win.

The point is to secure a victory, and the final innings are the most crucial ones. A guy who has thrown 100 or more pitches, no matter how well, is probably not going to be as effective as a fresh arm out of the bullpen.

The modern pitching staff is composed of starters, long relievers, middle relievers, short men, set-up men, a closer, and even a pitcher whose job is simply to get one batter out.

LEE SMITH *has saved more games—471 as we go to press—than any pitcher in baseball history. With his menacing glare and overpowering fastball, Smith has recorded at least 25 saves a year since 1983.*

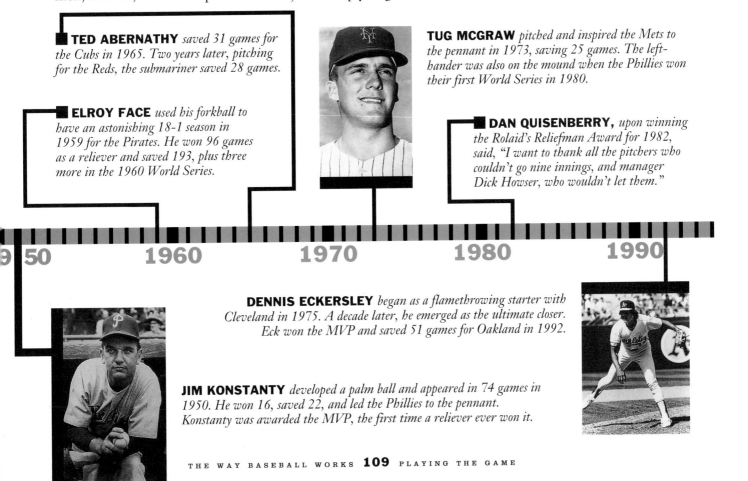

■ **TED ABERNATHY** *saved 31 games for the Cubs in 1965. Two years later, pitching for the Reds, the submariner saved 28 games.*

■ **ELROY FACE** *used his forkball to have an astonishing 18-1 season in 1959 for the Pirates. He won 96 games as a reliever and saved 193, plus three more in the 1960 World Series.*

TUG MCGRAW *pitched and inspired the Mets to the pennant in 1973, saving 25 games. The left-hander was also on the mound when the Phillies won their first World Series in 1980.*

■ **DAN QUISENBERRY,** *upon winning the Rolaid's Reliefman Award for 1982, said, "I want to thank all the pitchers who couldn't go nine innings, and manager Dick Howser, who wouldn't let them."*

9 50   1960   1970   1980   1990

DENNIS ECKERSLEY *began as a flamethrowing starter with Cleveland in 1975. A decade later, he emerged as the ultimate closer. Eck won the MVP and saved 51 games for Oakland in 1992.*

JIM KONSTANTY *developed a palm ball and appeared in 74 games in 1950. He won 16, saved 22, and led the Phillies to the pennant. Konstanty was awarded the MVP, the first time a reliever ever won it.*

"There's not much to it. You put a right-hand hitter against a left-hand pitcher and a left-hand hitter against a right-hand pitcher and on cloudy days you use a fastball pitcher."

—Casey Stengel

The **Platoon** *system*

CASEY STENGEL *was platooned himself when he had trouble hitting lefties for the Brooklyn Dodgers and New York Giants. The name "platoon" was borrowed from football, which was in the process of switching from a system in which players played both offense and defense to a system of two "platoons" for offense and defense.*

As soon as the game was invented, it became apparent that batters see the pitch better and hit better against opposite-handed pitchers. "Platooning," in which a right-hander and a left-hander share a slot in the batting order and play depending on who the opposing pitcher is, was pioneered by manager Cap Anson of the Chicago White Stockings in 1886. Platooning wasn't used widely until the 1950s, when Casey Stengel shuffled his Yankees like a deck of cards, making the most of his players' strengths. His players disliked being platooned, but there was no arguing with Stengel's success, and platooning became standard procedure.

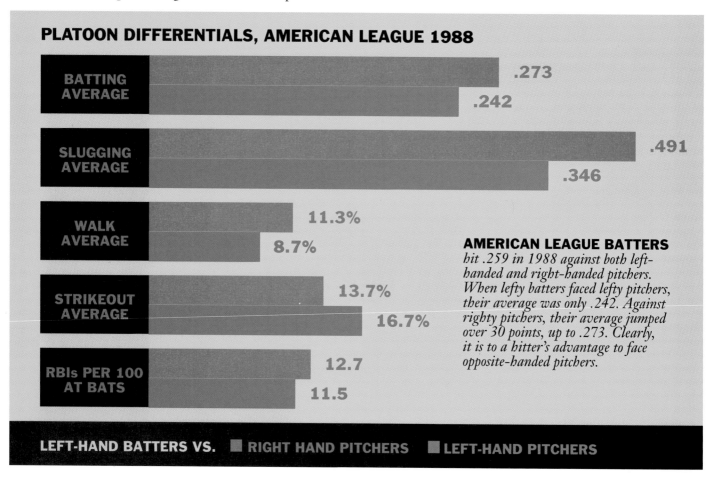

PLATOON DIFFERENTIALS, AMERICAN LEAGUE 1988

BATTING AVERAGE
.273
.242

SLUGGING AVERAGE
.491
.346

WALK AVERAGE
11.3%
8.7%

STRIKEOUT AVERAGE
13.7%
16.7%

RBIs PER 100 AT BATS
12.7
11.5

AMERICAN LEAGUE BATTERS *hit .259 in 1988 against both left-handed and right-handed pitchers. When lefty batters faced lefty pitchers, their average was only .242. Against righty pitchers, their average jumped over 30 points, up to .273. Clearly, it is to a hitter's advantage to face opposite-handed pitchers.*

LEFT-HAND BATTERS VS. ■ **RIGHT HAND PITCHERS** ■ **LEFT-HAND PITCHERS**

IF YOU CAN HIT *from both sides of the plate, you don't have to worry about being platooned or replaced by a pinch hitter. Mickey Mantle was the greatest switch hitter ever, slugging 373 homers left-handed and 163 right-handed. On ten occasions, Mantle hit homers both lefty and righty in the same game. Eddie Murray among others has also accomplished that feat.*

The greatest
Pinch Hitters

RON NORTHEY *pinch-hit three grand slams, more than anybody.*

SMOKY BURGESS *was a .286 pinch hitter, with 145 hits in 507 at bats.*

JERRY LYNCH *hit 18 pinch homers in his career.*

BERNIE CARBO *pinch-hit a dramatic three-run blast in the 1975 World Series.*

When the other team brings in an opposite-handed pitcher, managers scurry to revamp their batting order. If hitting a baseball is truly the most difficult thing to do in sport, pinch hitting must be the ultimate challenge. "Some of the game's greatest haven't been able to handle it," manager Ralph Houk once said. "Yet, men with .220 batting averages have been murder when sent up off the bench. I'll tell you this much: It's one of the toughest pressure jobs in baseball, because most of the time it means the ballgame."

MANNY MOTA *and his bat (right): 150 pinch hits, the career record.*

TED WILLIAMS *was a lefty pull hitter, so in 1946 Cleveland manager Lou Boudreau employed the "Williams shift"—stacking as many as six fielders in his right field hitting zone. Other teams used the shift against Williams, and for the most part, he refused to hit the ball the other way. Williams may have been hurt by the shift, but he was awesome nevertheless.*

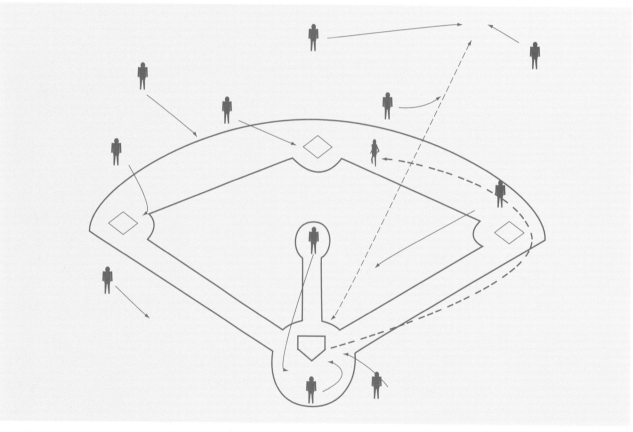

MORE THAN MEETS THE EYE *It's a common occurrence—a runner on first, a ball hit into the gap in right-center. While you're watching the ball bounce against the fence, every man on the field has a specific role he must play: the second baseman is running into shallow right field to take the throw from the outfielder. The shortstop is covering second base. The first baseman checks to see that the batter has touched that base, and then positions himself in the infield, about 25 feet in front of home plate, in the path of a throw to the plate; he's the cut-off man. The catcher covers home, prepared to block the plate. The pitcher runs behind home plate to back up any errant throws. The third baseman positions himself near the bag. The left fielder moves in, ready to back up either second or third base. On the offense, the third base coach runs halfway toward home, and will signal the runner from first whether to try and score or not; if he sends the runner, he'll then direct the batter to stay at second or try for third. The on deck batter moves toward the plate and will signal the runner coming home to slide or stay up. The first base coach will direct the batter to stay at first or go on to second. Among the many subsequent scenarios: a collision at home, or perhaps the first baseman will cut off the relay throw and fire the ball to the shortstop to try and get the batter at second base.*

"The phrase 'off with the crack of the bat,' while romantic, is really meaningless, since the outfielder should be in motion long before he hears the sound of the ball meeting the bat."

—Joe DiMaggio

The department of
Defense

For nine players to cover a field the size of a city block, they need good reaction time, strong arms, speed up the middle, good hands, and—the most important thing—brains.

There are so many situations in which positioning the fielders can influence the outcome of a game. If a hitter always hits the ball to left field, it stands to reason that fielders should be concentrated there. A pitch thrown inside is likely to be pulled, so the fielders should be shaded to one side. Hitters often swing late against power pitchers, so the defense should be shaded to the opposite side. Late in a close game, the foul lines should be guarded to prevent extra base hits. If a runner at third is in a position to score the game-winning run, the infield will move in to try and nail him at the plate. With two outs, the third baseman need not play close because a bunt is unlikely. These are defensive fundamentals.

The score, the inning, the count, the presence of base runners, the ability of the hitter and pitcher, and sometimes the wind, sun, or dimensions of the ballpark all influence how those nine players should cover the field.

HUNG OUT TO DRY *With the runner caught between two bases, the defense wants to run the ball toward him at full speed, make him commit to moving backwards, and then throw the ball to the baseman to apply the tag. Ideally, one throw should be all that is necessary to nail the runner. The more the ball is tossed back and forth, the greater chance an error will be made.*

ON ANY BALL *hit to the right side of the diamond, pitchers are instructed to break for first. If the first baseman has to field the ball and cannot then run to the bag to beat the runner, he will flip the ball to the pitcher covering.*

POP FLIES *hit between the infield and the outfield can be an adventure. To avoid collisions, fielders must communicate with each other to make it clear who has the best chance of making the play.*

ALAN TRAMMELL AND LOU WHITAKER *of the Detroit Tigers formed a "keystone combination" for 1,918 games through 1995, many more than any other two players. The two began their partnership in the minor leagues.*

Two birds with one stone:

The Double Play

A SLOW RUNNER *is easy to double up. In one unfortunate game in 1975, Joe Torre (above) of the Mets hit into four double plays. That feat was also accomplished by Goose Goslin and Mike Kreevich.*

Getting two outs on one batted ball brings a smile to the face of any manager, at least when his team is in the field. The double play is a great rally killer and a ballet for fans to watch. There are plenty of ways to "turn two," but a typical 6-4-3 (a shortstop-second baseman-first baseman) twin killing goes like this: With a runner on first, the batter hits a sharp but easily fieldable grounder to the left side. The shortstop scoops the ball cleanly and quickly flips it, chest height, to his second baseman. The second baseman, sprinting toward the bag, deftly touches it with his foot as he receives the ball, pivots, and whips a strong, accurate throw to first as he leaps out of the way of the charging base runner. The first baseman stretches for the ball just before the runner crosses the bag. There's only one thing more elegant than a double play—a triple play.

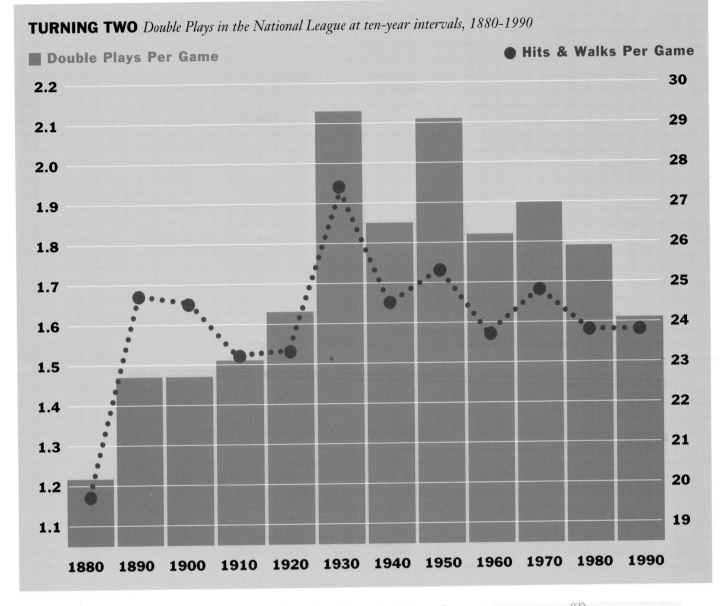

TURNING TWO *Double Plays in the National League at ten-year intervals, 1880-1990*

■ **Double Plays Per Game**

● **Hits & Walks Per Game**

(Left axis values, top to bottom: 2.2, 2.1, 2.0, 1.9, 1.8, 1.7, 1.6, 1.5, 1.4, 1.3, 1.2, 1.1)

(Right axis values, top to bottom: 30, 29, 28, 27, 26, 25, 24, 23, 22, 21, 20, 19)

(X axis: 1880, 1890, 1900, 1910, 1920, 1930, 1940, 1950, 1960, 1970, 1980, 1990)

POETRY IN MOTION *"These are the saddest of possible words: Tinker to Evers to Chance," wrote Franklin P. Adams in 1910. In fact, shortstop Joe Tinker, second baseman Johnny Evers, and first baseman Frank Chance didn't turn nearly as many DPs as most infields do today, but they brought the Cubs to the World Series in 1906, 1907, 1908, and 1910. They had the help of third baseman Harry Steinfeldt, whose biggest liability was that his name did not lend itself to poetry.*

THE WIZARD OF OZ
St. Louis Cardinal Ozzie Smith (left) is one of the best shortstops ever, with a raft of records for chances, assists, double plays, and fielding average. Ozzie once helped turn six double plays in a single game.

Winners of the **Gold Glove**

The home-run hitter and the strike-out pitcher grab the headlines, but great fielders win ballgames too. An airtight defense prevents runs, keeps a team in the game, and gives the players the emotional boost they need to score runs.

Great plays don't show up in the box score or the headlines. When a third baseman snares a rocket down the line that would have gone for a double, all he gets is a putout. When a centerfielder throws a runner out at the plate, all he gets is an assist. When a catcher blocks a pitch in the dirt or a rightfielder throws a bullet to third base and the runner dashes back to second, all they get is respect.

And perhaps a trophy. The Gold Glove Award is given to a player at each position in each league who has been voted the best fielder that season. Here we celebrate the nine players who have won the most Gold Gloves since the award began in 1957.

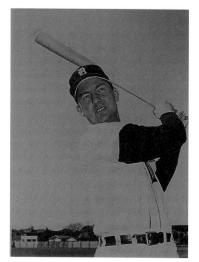

AL KALINE (right) never played a day in the minors, and never played right field until he was sent out there in his first major league game as a 19-year-old kid. It seemed to suit him. Kaline had a great arm, the quickness of an infielder, and would go on to win 10 Gold Gloves.

SHORTSTOP: OZZIE SMITH won 13 Gold Gloves in a row with San Diego and St. Louis, diving for balls, bouncing off the dirt and throwing on the run with grace that is seen more in ballet than in baseball. His records are too numerous to list here.

THIRD BASE: BROOKS ROBINSON was the human vacuum cleaner. Robinson made simply unbelievable plays, earning him 16 straight Gold Gloves. He holds lifetime records at third base for fielding average, putouts, assists, chances, and double plays. Robinson practically won the 1970 World Series singlehandedly with his glove work.

WILLIE MAYS *had the ability to catch an uncatchable ball and then throw a bullet to nail the astonished baserunner desperately trying to return to his base. On easier plays, Mays used his "basket catch." The "Say Hey Kid" won a dozen Gold Gloves and would have won more but he already had five seasons under his belt when the award was introduced.*

ROBERTO CLEMENTE *also won a dozen Gold Gloves. Clemente could track down anything in right field that didn't go over the fence, and quite a few that did. After leading the league in assists five times, his arm was the most feared in baseball and few runners dared take an extra base on him.*

SECOND BASE: RYNE SANDBERG *set a National League record with only five errors in 1986 and a fielding average of .9938. In 1989 he set another record by going 90 games at second base without an error. All together, "Ryno" won nine Gold Gloves in a row during his years with the Cubs.*

FIRST BASE: KEITH HERNANDEZ *redefined the first baseman's role. "Mex" won 11 straight Gold Gloves from 1978 to 1988, during which he led the league in double plays six times, assists five times, putouts four times, and fielding average twice.*

PITCHER: JIM KAAT *moved like a cat, lapping up 16 Gold Gloves in a row with Twins, White Sox, and Phillies. "Kitty" pitched for a quarter of a century, averaging only 2.2 errors a year.*

CATCHER: JOHNNY BENCH'S *arm was a gun, and he would have thrown out many more base stealers if they had been foolish enough to run on him. Bench won 10 Gold Gloves in a row as he led The "Big Red Machine" to six division titles and two World Championships in the 1970s. He set records for durability (catching over 100 games for his first 13 seasons) and popularized one-handed catching.*

THE AMAZIN' METS *lost an amazin' number of games, averaging 108 losses a year for their first six years. Their five starting pitchers combined for a 30-92 record in 1962, with two of them losing 20 games apiece. Still, the 40-120 Mets could feel good in comparison to the 1899 Cleveland Spiders, who won just 20 games and lost 134.*

CONNIE MACK *won nine pennants and five World Series during his managing career, but he also finished dead last 17 times and Philadelphia lost 249 more games than they won under his command. Mack owed his longevity as a manager to the fact that he also owned the team. His modus operandi was to sell off his star players as soon as the team achieved greatness. "It is more profitable," Mack said, "for me to have a team that is in contention for most of the season but finishes about fourth."*

Wait 'til Next Year

Failure is a big part of baseball, sometimes a larger part than we realize. Ty Cobb, the greatest hitter in history, failed to get a hit 7,245 times he came to the plate. His average for *not* hitting, in fact, was a sparkling .633. Nolan Ryan, undoubtedly one of the game's great pitchers, only won 32 more games than he lost. Christy Mathewson, with his pinpoint pitching control, walked 838 batters. Babe Ruth struck out 1,330 times. One of baseball's greatest managers, John McGraw lost 1,959 games. Ozzie Smith booted over 200 balls.

A ballplayer's overwhelming rate of failure and occasional success reminds us of ourselves. We urge him on, no matter how futile or pathetic he is. Marv Throneberry, seen here, epitomized the lovable loser, stumbling, bumbling, and winning the hearts of fans as he led the newborn New York Mets straight to the cellar in 1962. Marvelous Marv became a cult hero, and like losers before him (Bob Uecker, Fred Merkle, the Cubs) fans couldn't help but root for the underdog in hopes that someday he might come out on top. We are hopeless optimists. No matter how bad things get, we always remember the battle cry of Brooklyn Dodger fans—"Wait 'til next year!"

THE MENDOZA LINE *hovers around .200, the average at which hitters should seriously consider other career alternatives. The phrase was coined by George Brett in honor of good fielding shortstop Mario Mendoza, who hit below .200 five times in nine years with the Pirates, Mariners, and Rangers. (Actually, Mendoza averaged .215 and hit a respectable .245 in 1980.) The Baseball Encyclopedia lists two other Mendozas, and they were even worse hitters than Mario.*

"I know that many tremendous multi-sports athletes who crushed fastballs over the fences in the minors quit baseball soon after confronting the major league curveball. I was told when I was in the minors that it would be easier hitting in the majors because the lighting was better and the pitchers were always around the plate. But that didn't take into account the unpredictability of major league pitchers. I was shocked that Juan Marichal would throw a screwball on a 3-0 count with the bases loaded."

—**Tim McCarver**

MICHAEL JORDAN *found it a lot easier to shoot a big rubber ball into a hoop than to hit minor league fastballs. Jordan barely made it past the Mendoza Line, hitting .202 for the AA Birmingham Barons in 1994, striking out once every four times at bat, with 11 widely publicized errors in the field. After one season he went back to being the greatest basketball player who ever lived.*

DRINKING PROBLEM *Al "Fuzzy" Smith of the White Sox didn't ask for a beer, but he got one after a homer sailed into the stands during the 1959 World Series. The Dodgers beat the Sox four games to two. Smith was not popular with Chicago fans after the team traded Minnie Minoso to get him. To win them over, the Sox held an Al Smith Night, in which anyone named Smith was admitted free and given a button that read, "I'm a Smith and I'm for Al."*

THE WAY BASEBALL WORKS **120** PLAYING THE GAME

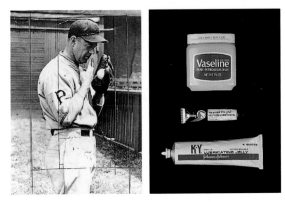

"One of the few things about baseball that hasn't changed since the turn of the century is the fact that pitchers cheat."

—Umpire Ron Luciano

THE SPITBALL *was invented by George Hildebrand in 1902 and elevated to an art by Gaylord Perry. Perry (opposite), "The King of Grease," admitted putting everything from fishing line wax to suntan lotion on the ball and even titled his autobiography, "Me and the Spitter." The pitch was banned in 1920, but pitchers who had already used the spitball were allowed to keep throwing it until they were out of baseball. Burleigh Grimes (above) was the last pitcher to throw a legal spitball when he retired in 1934.*

Rule bending: **Pitchers**

In baseball, it isn't necessary to weigh a defensive lineman's 300 pounds or tower over your opponents like a seven-foot center. It's a game for normal-size athletes (6-foot-10-inch Randy Johnson notwithstanding) who rely on their talent and wits. The game lends itself to ingenuity, clever deception, and resourcefulness, qualities we admire in competitors of any sport.

Many pitchers throw spitballs or scuffballs. The spitter is thrown by putting moisture on the ball or on the fingers so that the ball can be thrown with little rotation. The scuffball means physically damaging a baseball—with whatever tools on hand—to disrupt the airflow and make it break dramatically. Both pitches are illegal, but enforcement is lax. In fact, two admitted experts—Whitey Ford and Gaylord Perry—are enshrined in the Baseball Hall of Fame.

THE SCUFFBALL *was invented by Russ Ford in 1910 and perfected by Whitey Ford (far right, no relation to Russ) and his partner in crime catcher Elston Howard (bottom, right). When Ford needed a big out, he would rough up the ball with a sharpened ring, or Howard would use his shinguard. Rick Honeycutt (top, right) was even more blatant. In 1980, he was caught with a thumbtack sticking through a Band-Aid on his finger.*

HITTERS ONCE BELIEVED *they could hit the ball farther if their bats were heavier. Cincinnati Reds slugger Ted Kluszewski (above) would bang 10-penny nails into his bats. George Sisler used Victrola needles. Other hitters have slammed their bats with sledgehammers, peeled away the wood to make one side flat, scraped out the soft grain of the wood, and carved grooves to put backspin on the ball.*

"When a guy who has never hit more than 10 home runs in the major leagues suddenly hits 40, you've got to question how much of that is the result of working out and how much is due to other causes. In my opinion, when totals like that go into the books, there ought to be an asterisk next to them and the word cheating in parentheses."

—Ozzie Smith

Rule Bending:
Batters

Batters don't have as many opportunities at their disposal to bend the rules as pitchers do. For the most part they hollow out their bats to make them an ounce or two lighter, enabling them to swing faster, and therefore hit the ball farther.

Why don't they simply use a lighter bat? There are only two ways to make a bat lighter. You can cut it down so it is shorter, or you can shave wood off the barrel or handle to make it thinner. In either case, you have a smaller weapon with less hitting surface. By hollowing out the inside of the bat, you can take off the weight without making the bat any smaller. Some players insist on corking their bat but many experts believe the advantage it gives a hitter is purely psychological.

THE MOST FAMOUS LOADED BAT INCIDENT *took place on September 7, 1974. Graig Nettles of the Yankees (left) hit a home run in the first game of a doubleheader and another one in the second inning of the second game. In the fifth inning, he hit an opposite field single and six rubber Super Balls flew out of his bat. That week* Time *magazine reported, "Nettles was the first man to bounce out to the third baseman, the shortstop, and the second baseman all at once."*

HOW TO CORK A BAT *First you bore a hole one inch in diameter about a foot into the barrel. Clean out the hole and pack it with cork, Styrofoam, or something that is lighter than wood (to avoid a hollow sound). Next, plug the hole with plastic wood the same color as the bat. Sand the top smooth, smear on some pine tar to cover any lines, and you're ready to sock one out of the park. Admitted corker Norm Cash (above) demonstrates the form he might have used to hit .361 and win the American League batting title in 1961.*

"I'm not concerned with your liking or disliking me...All I ask is that you respect me as a human being."

—Jackie Robinson

Breaking the
Color Barrier

It seems unthinkable today that for sixty years major league baseball refused to admit qualified players because of the color of their skin. Besides being grossly unfair to a race of people, the color barrier also cheated Major League Baseball fans of all races out of the chance to witness the talents of Josh Gibson, Cool Papa Bell, Oscar Charleston,

Ray Dandridge, Buck Leonard, Judy Johnson, and so many other players in the Negro League. Racism didn't disappear when Jackie Robinson stepped to the plate for the first time in 1947, but it would never recover. Robinson's determination and dignity paved the way for the stars who would follow him— Henry Aaron, Willie Mays, Frank Robinson, Bob Gibson, Maury Wills, Ernie Banks, Rickey Henderson, Joe Morgan, Reggie Jackson, Tony Gwynn, Eddie Murray, Willie Stargell, Ozzie Smith, Barry Bonds, Frank Thomas, and Ken Griffey Jr. to name a few.

PIONEERS *Moses Fleetwood Walker (inset left) was the first black major leaguer, playing for Toledo in the American Association in 1884. Chicago White Stockings manager Cap Anson (above) refused to let his team take the field if Walker was on it, and up went the color barrier in 1887. Dodger GM Branch Rickey decided that Jackie Robinson (opposite) was the player to break the barrier. Jackie was chosen not just because of the quality of his play but also because of the strength of his character.*

JOSH GIBSON AND RUBE FOSTER *didn't live to see the day the color barrier was eliminated. But Gibson (far left) was still perhaps the greatest slugger the game has known, hitting an estimated 823 home runs in his Negro League career while averaging .384. Foster (left) was a crafty and dominating pitcher who went on to found the Negro National League in 1920, laying the foundation that would later enable black players to play in the majors. Both men eventually made it to the Hall of Fame.*

A timeline of Trouble and Tragedy

Baseball, like society, has never been squeaky clean. However, only in recent decades has the public learned that a few of the game's stars have not always been perfect role models.

Fortunately, fans are coming around to the understanding that baseball is too good a game to be ruined by the acts of a small minority of the men who play and run it. When the Black Sox purposely lost the 1919 World Series for money, the game went on. When the players and owners cancelled the 1994 World Series for money, the game went on. The game went on when we found out that Ty Cobb and Mickey Mantle might not have led perfect lives off the field, the game went on. The game even went on when the players and owners cancelled the 1994 World Series in a dispute over money.

1877 LOUISVILLE GRAYS *Four players banned for life for throwing games.*

1882 DICK HIGHAM *National League umpire caught fixing games and was banned for life.*

1894 TERRY LARKIN *National League umpire caught fixing games and was banned for life.*

1887 COLOR BARRIER *Cap Anson of the Chicago White Stockings refuses to take the field if a black player is on it. It would be a whites-only game for 60 years.*

"I won over two hundred games, but what happened to me in August of 1920 is the only thing anybody remembers."

—**Carl Mays,** *on the errant pitch that resulted in the death of Ray Chapman*

1920 RAY CHAPMAN *The shortstop of the Cleveland Indians is the only major league player killed by a pitched ball.*

1912 TY COBB *Angry at the world, the Georgia Peach charges into the stands and beats up a handicapped heckler.*

70 1880s 1890s 1900s 1910s

THE 1919 CHICAGO WHITE SOX *gave baseball its worst black eye when eight players allegedly threw the World Series for money.*

1927 TY COBB & TRIS SPEAKER *(above)*
Two of the game's greatest players are accused—and eventually acquitted—of betting on a game they played in.

1972 ROBERTO CLEMENTE
Pittsburgh's superstar goes down in a plane crash while bringing medicine and food to survivors of an earthquake in Nicaragua.

1974 BEER NIGHT *Cleveland fans get loaded on ten cent beer and riot, setting off cherry bombs and attacking players on the Texas Rangers.*

1985 DRUGS *Seven players are suspended because they had "in some fashion facilitated the distribution of drugs in baseball."*

1964 KEN HUBBS *The National League Rookie of the Year is killed in a plane crash at the age of 22.*

1947 LEO DUROCHER
The fiery Dodger man-ager is suspended for a year for consorting with gamblers.

20 **1930** **1940** **1950** **1960** **1970** **1980**

1965 MARICHAL-ROSEBORO *Giant pitcher brutally attacks the Dodger catcher with a bat.*

1979 THURMAN MUNSON *The MVP catcher crashes his plane near Canton, Ohio.*

1989 PETE ROSE *The game's all-time hit leader denies that he bet on baseball games, but agrees to a lifetime ban.*

1949 EDDIE WAITKUS
A deranged fan stalks and shoots the Phillie first baseman.

1979 BILLY MARTIN
The hotheaded Yankee manager gets into his most celebrated fight, with marshmallow salesman Joseph Cooper.

A TALE OF THREE SEASONS: 1910, 1950, 1990

Phil Rizzuto's sparkling play won him the 1950 AL MVP award, and his Yankees swept the Phillies in the World Series.

HITS PER GAME

1910	16.3
1950	18.2
1990	17.5

RUNS PER GAME

1910	7.7
1950	9.7
1990	8.5

PROBABILITY OF A COMPLETE GAME

1910	62%
1950	40%
1990	10%

STEALS PER GAME

1910	2.6
1950	0.5
1990	1.6

Mordecai "Three Finger" Brown racked up 25 wins and 7 shutouts for the 1910 NL Champion Cubs.

ERRORS PER GAME

1910	3.6
1950	1.9
1990	1.5

ATTENDANCE

1910	4,969
1950	14,105
1990	26,045

NUMBER OF PITCHERS USED

1910	2.8
1950	4.2
1990	6.0

DOUBLES PER GAME

1910	2.25
1950	3
1990	3.1

TRIPLES PER GAME

1910	0.9
1950	0.6
1990	0.4

Jose Canseco swatted 37 homers for the Oakland A's, who won their third straight AL title in 1990.

HOME RUNS PER GAME

1910	0.3
1950	1.7
1990	1.6

STRIKEOUTS AS A PERCENTAGE OF ALL OUTS

1910	14.4%
1950	14.5%
1990	21.1%

How the Game has Changed

Baseball has a reputation for being a timeless, proudly traditional game that has hardly changed since it was invented long ago in some long ago cow pasture. The truth is that baseball in its present form is almost unrecognizable from the original game. Most of the games are at night now, and many are played indoors on artificial grass. Teams now have ten players on each side in the American League, and they represent all races. In 1900 it was whites only and there was no American League. The bat is lighter and thinner now. The glove is larger. The ball is livelier. The uniforms are tighter. The season is longer. The field is smaller, but ballpark capacity is larger. Beanballs are rarer, but charging the mound is more common. Doubleheaders are gone. The players can make as much money as the owners now, and are no longer legally bound to a team for life. Some of these changes were for the better, some for the worse. Through it all, the game lives on.

IT'S A FAN'S FANTASY *If you could travel through time and see a typical 1910 game in the morning, a 1950 game in the afternoon, and a 1990 game at night, what would you see? On the surface, the three games will look similar—three strikes, three outs, nine innings, and nine fielders. But there would be big differences. You might see at least one pitcher throw a complete game in the morning and afternoon, but not at your night game. You'll see a lot more errors in the morning than you'll see later in the day, but fewer double plays and hardly any homers. You'll see more strikeouts at your night game, and fewer triples. Finally, you'll see lots of stolen bases in the morning, hardly ANY in the afternoon, and more again at night.*

BUCOLIC BALLPARKS • WOOD, CONCRETE, AND STEEL
DIMENSIONS • STADIUMS & STATS • ASTROTURF
INDOOR BASEBALL • COOKIE CUTTERS & THROWBACKS
FAMILIAR FIGURES • A FAMILY OF GROUNDSKEEPERS
SCOREBOARDS, BILLBOARDS, AND CLEANING UP

*Scoreboard operator,
Yankee Stadium*

*Seat from the
Polo Grounds*

Chapter Four

Imagine if each football field was different. Or if some basketball courts were 94 feet long, others 150. Or if some hockey rinks were rectangles, while others were parallelograms. Sports would be chaos.

Football fields, basketball courts, and hockey rinks are standardized all over the world. A tennis court in Queens has the exact same dimensions as one in Wimbledon. But baseball specifically and purposefully constructs each of its venues differently from every other one.

The field of play forces players to make adjustments depending upon where they're playing. A shot off the "Green Monster" in Fenway Park will bounce differently from the same hit off the wall in Toronto's SkyDome. Fans can wonder and argue whether a double would be a home run in another park or whether a player would have had better numbers if he played for another team. In fact, a player may be traded because his skills do not fit the dimensions of the team's field.

The ballpark, then, adds a level of complexity to the game, a charming wrinkle that would seem ridiculous in other sports but is simply accepted in baseball. Oh, to be back in the Polo Grounds, which was once 258 feet down the right field line and 500 feet to centerfield!

Busch Stadium

Toronto's Skydome

The Ballpark

Alexander Cartwright

Ebbets Field

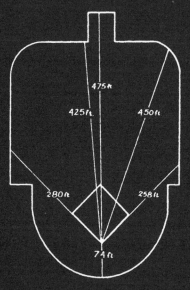
475 ft

425 ft   450 ft

280 ft   258 ft

74 ft

Polo Grounds

Marshall Bossard

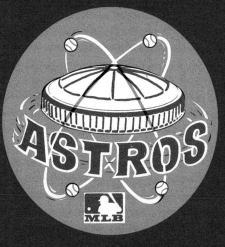
ASTROS
MLB

THE CIVIL WAR *helped popularize baseball, as soldiers on both sides taught their buddies the new game. In 1862 two Union teams played before 40,000 people at Hilton Head, South Carolina. On their way home from Appomattox, the New York Volunteers and Washington Nationals played a game behind the White House.*

"Decades after a person has stopped collecting bubble gum cards, he can still discover himself collecting ballparks . . . their smells, their special seasons, their moods."

—Thomas Boswell

The First *ballparks*

Baseball is considered a pastoral game, but it grew up on the streets of New York City. One of the first organized teams, the New York Knickerbockers, started practicing at 26th Street in Manhattan, a site which would one day be the first Madison Square Garden. The crowded city streets prompted the Knickerbockers to move across the Hudson River and play at Elysian Fields in Hoboken, New Jersey.

Hoboken in the 1840s, believe it or not, was a rural tourist attraction for stressed-out New Yorkers. Alexander Cartwright and his pals would take the ferry (13 cents) across the river after work every Tuesday and Friday afternoon. Cartwright is widely credited with drawing up the rules to the game and his Knickerbocker Club, formed in 1845, was among the first to play the game.

PLAY FOR PAY *Ballparks were first enclosed by fences mainly to enable teams to charge money to watch their games. This 1871 poster advertises an upcoming game of the Eagle Baseball Club. With admission being paid players demanded a share of the gate, and baseball became a professional sport.*

They were soundly trounced, 23-1, suggesting that either the New York Nine were really the first organized team, or that the Knickerbockers were the first disorganized team.

In any case, amateur gentlemen like the Knickerbockers took up the new game in neighboring towns along the East Coast. They played for the exercise, in open fields. They called themselves "clubs," not "teams." There were no stands, and no admission was charged.

By the 1860s, the natural human desire to win had replaced exercise as the main motivation to play baseball. Teams started acquiring out-of-town players to improve themselves. Soon, the best players were being slipped money to entice them to join a team. This was shocking at the time, but inevitable. Baseball was changing from a recreational sport into a business.

Money to pay players had to come from somewhere, and it made sense to charge the hundreds of people who were gathering to watch the games.

Brooklyn politician William Cammeyer is known as "the father of the enclosed ballpark." On May 15, 1862, he opened The Union Grounds in Brooklyn on the site of an ice-skating rink. The field featured something new—a fence. Eventually, fences would be moved in, the ball livened, and homers plentiful.

More importantly for Cammeyer, the fence kept out the riff-raff who wouldn't pay 10 cents to watch a baseball game.

ELYSIAN FIELDS *One of the first recorded games took place in Hoboken, New Jersey, on June 19, 1846. Notice that the first, second, and third basemen positioned themselves right on their bases. In 1938, a Maxwell House Coffee plant was built on the site.*

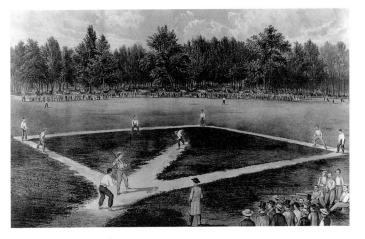

"A portion of the building attached to the cheap seats gave way just as the game closed. The spectators occupying that part of the grounds were hurrying, as is usual, to get outside and catch a street-car. As they passed along the south-east end of the 'bleaching board' and came down on the steps there was a loud crack, and the next instant about twenty feet of platform caved in. Between fifty and sixty people were precipitated to the ground."

—The Cincinnati Enquirer, *May 2, 1884,*

after the bleachers collapsed at American Ball Park on Opening Day

The Union Grounds seated 1,500, including benches for ladies and a special section exclusively for gamblers. A band even played "The Star-Spangled Banner" before games.

BOX SEATS *The horses and buggies of wealthy fans who came to the Polo Grounds in 1903 formed a ring around the outfield.*

After the Civil War, enclosed stadiums—made from wood—popped up in most large cities. They were usually on the outskirts of urban areas, where land was affordable and there was room to park horses and buggies. Some of these fields were quite elaborate. Chicago's West Side Park opened in 1885, sporting a dozen rooftop luxury boxes.

Ballparks of that era didn't usually have a clubhouse for the visiting team. They would dress in their uniforms at the hotel and parade to the park in open carriages, sometimes accompanied by marching bands. This served to create interest in the day's game, and also allowed the locals to hurl opinions—and fruit—at visiting players.

In these old ballparks, fans watched from their cars, from trees, poles, and fences. When there was a big crowd, they would be herded into the outfield, where they could watch the game from behind a rope. Naturally, the rope would be pushed forward

THE GRAND PAVILION *in Boston in the 1880s.*

when the home team was up, and back when the visitors came to bat. Balls hit into the crowd became ground rule doubles.

Unfortunately, these wooden stadiums had a disturbing tendency to collapse or burn down, sometimes in the middle of a game. In 1894 alone, fires ruined National League parks in Baltimore, Philadelphia, Boston, and Chicago.

When the main grandstand of Eclipse Park in Louisville burned to the ground in 1899 and the Colonels were dropped from the National League, Louisville owner Barney Dreyfuss purchased another league franchise and took his best players— Honus Wagner, Rube Waddell, and Fred Clarke—to Pittsburgh.

On March 1, 1909, ground was broken to build Forbes Field, named in honor of General John Forbes, a hero of the French and Indian War. Dreyfuss hauled in 40 carloads of structural steel and 110 carloads of cement. A new era of ballparks had begun.

WRIGLEY FIELD *opened on April 23, 1914. The Cubs' owners resisted night baseball, introduced in 1935, for more than 50 years, until lights were finally installed and the first official night game took place at Wrigley on August 9, 1988.*

YANKEE STADIUM'S *centerfield (also known as "Death Valley") was so far away from home plate that monuments to Babe Ruth, Lou Gehrig, and Miller Huggins were placed in fair territory out there. Gehrig's monument (above) was dedicated a month after he passed away in 1941. The program from the first game at Yankee Stadium, April 18, 1923 (left).*

Classic *ballparks*

Baseball was exploding in popularity at the turn of the century. So was America. Railroad tracks and telegraph lines sprouted up everywhere. Immigrants and former slaves streamed into the cities. Bigger, fireproof ballparks were needed.

These new parks—made from structural steel and reinforced concrete—were built in the middle of cities, at the intersections of rail and trolley lines. They had to be shoehorned in to fit the shape of the existing surrounding streets. This forced ballpark designers to create irregularly shaped fields with upper decks, slopes, high and low walls, and other idiosyncrasies that gave each ballpark a unique personality.

Today we view many of the concrete-and-steel ballparks built from 1909 to 1923 as "classics," and their quirky dimensions helped change the game. Of necessity, the inner city parks were often smaller than the ones they replaced. Baseball became more offensive and hitters began to swing for the fences. The home-run era was on its way.

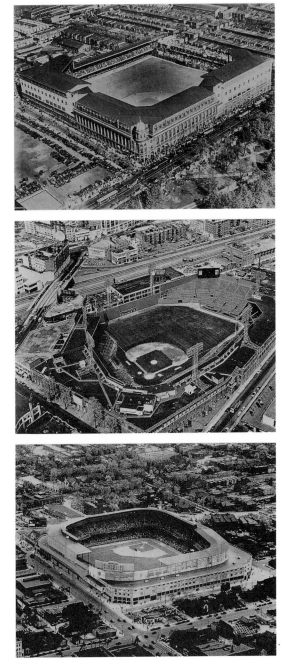

THREE "CLASSIC PARKS" *opened between 1909 and 1912: Shibe Park (top) was home for the Phillies and Athletics and had a corrugated iron right-field fence, which caused balls to bounce in crazy directions. Boston's Fenway Park (middle) is most famous for the Green Monster, a 37-foot high wall in left field. Home plate and the batter's box at Tiger Stadium (bottom) are pointed slightly toward right field instead of directly toward the pitcher's mound, throwing visiting hitters and pitchers off stride.*

A SEAT *from the Polo Grounds, which, from 1923 on, featured a centerfield fence almost 500 feet from home plate.*

Park **Effects**

If Babe Ruth had hit his "called shot" homer in the oval-shaped Polo Grounds instead of at the square-format Wrigley Field, it probably would have been a routine fly ball out. Similarly, if Willie Mays had attempted "the catch" (below) in Wrigley instead of the Polo Grounds, the drive would have been a homer.

Many of baseball's classic moments occurred because the quirks of the particular ballpark enabled them to happen. They also allowed fans to wage lifelong arguments over what might have been. No one will ever know how many homers Ted Williams would have hit if he played in Yankee Stadium.

CANDLESTICK PARK *slants toward San Francisco Bay, which prompted its nickname "Cave of the Winds." The stadium is so windy that in the ninth inning of the 1961 All-Star Game, Giant pitcher Stu Miller was blown right off the mound (he was called for a balk). When the stadium was enclosed in 1971, the wind got even worse, swirling around like a tornado. That's not quite as bad as an earthquake, which disrupted the World Series here in 1989.*

THE HOUSE THAT RUTH BUILT *should have been called "The House That Was Built for Ruth." Yankee owner Jacob Ruppert had Yankee Stadium (above) designed with a short right field fence (295 feet) so Babe Ruth would hit home runs there. Ruth did, and the fans dubbed the right field stands "Ruthville." Similarly, Pittsburgh put up chicken coop wire in left field to create "Greenberg Gardens" for Hank Greenberg to aim at, and the Red Sox shortened the distance to the right field fence at Fenway to create "Williamsburg" for Ted Williams.*

FENWAY PARK *in Boston is most famous for its Green Monster, but it has other charms. Duffy's Cliff, a 10-foot incline, graced the bottom of that wall until 1933. It was named after Red Sox left fielder Duffy Lewis, who played it so well. Before 1970, there was a flagpole that was considered in play. Fenway has the smallest foul territory of any big-league park, which puts the fans (only 34,000) right in the action. The Green Monster has a ladder on it (which is in play) and a net at the top to catch home-run balls so they don't smash windows on Lansdowne Street.*

TIGER STADIUM *in Detroit opened the same day as Fenway—April 20, 1912. It was the first major-league park to have a background—a blank green wall—to help hitters see the ball. The upper deck hangs over the lower deck in right field by 10 feet, so it is possible to hit a 325-foot line drive that is caught and a 315 high fly that goes for a home run. One quirk—there used to be a 125-foot flagpole in centerfield that was in play.*

DODGER STADIUM *in Los Angeles is a pitcher's dream, with deep fences, lots of foul ground, and air that doesn't seem to like to carry a baseball. In its first four years, five Cy Young Awards were won by pitchers who called Dodger Stadium home (Sandy Koufax three times, Don Drysdale, and Dean Chance of the Los Angeles Angels). When it opened in 1962, somebody discovered the foul poles were in foul territory (oddly, foul poles are supposed to be in play). They stayed that way all season.*

Oh, yeah? **Prove It!**

I t's difficult to prove anything in baseball because so many factors get tangled together. Rules change over the years. Styles and trends change. New pitches are developed. Ballparks are shaped differently. Balls have become livelier; bats lighter; athletes, bigger and stronger. Trying to tease out essential truths from all this can be frustrating, and, at the same time, fascinating. That's what makes the game so interesting.

GOOD FIELD; NO HIT *The chart (right) shows that when the Dodgers moved to Chavez Ravine in 1962, their home runs and runs-per-game dropped like a spitball on a damp day. The ballpark is clearly a pitcher's park, as can be seen when compared with a hitter's park like Chicago's Wrigley Field (below).*

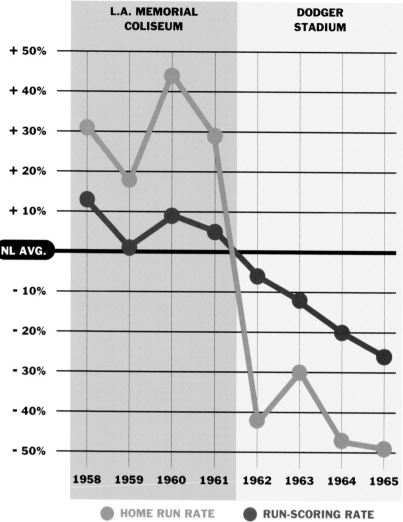

L.A. MEMORIAL COLISEUM — **DODGER STADIUM**

+ 50%
+ 40%
+ 30%
+ 20%
+ 10%
NL AVG.
- 10%
- 20%
- 30%
- 40%
- 50%

1958 1959 1960 1961 1962 1963 1964 1965

● HOME RUN RATE   ● RUN-SCORING RATE

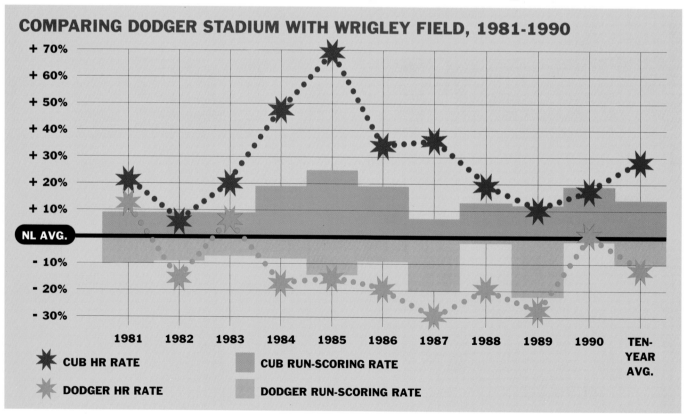

COMPARING DODGER STADIUM WITH WRIGLEY FIELD, 1981-1990

+ 70%
+ 60%
+ 50%
+ 40%
+ 30%
+ 20%
+ 10%
NL AVG.
- 10%
- 20%
- 30%

1981 1982 1983 1984 1985 1986 1987 1988 1989 1990 TEN-YEAR AVG.

✶ CUB HR RATE   CUB RUN-SCORING RATE

✶ DODGER HR RATE   DODGER RUN-SCORING RATE

CUB HR RATE
DODGER HR RATE
CUB RUN-SCORING RATE
DODGER RUN-SCORING RATE

WHO WAS BETTER? *This chart compares runs-per-game in Yankee Stadium and Fenway Park for the 10 years "Joltin' Joe" and "Teddy Ballgame" competed against each other. Williams enjoyed an obvious advantage playing in Fenway, and would finish his career with higher batting and slugging averages, more homers, hits, doubles, and RBIs.*

* Red indicates player led the AL in that category

Runs-per-Game Compared to AL Average, 1939-42 and 1946-51

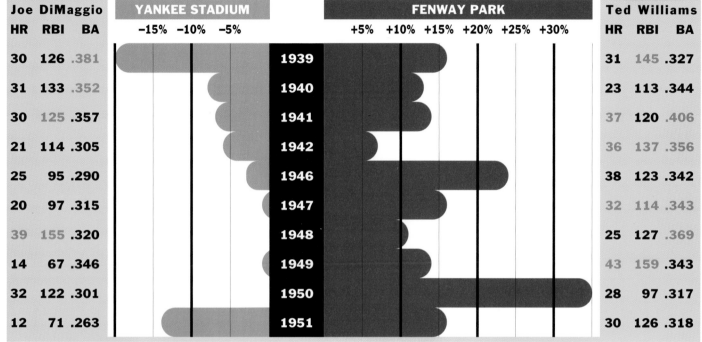

Joe DiMaggio			YANKEE STADIUM	FENWAY PARK	Ted Williams		
HR	RBI	BA	−15% −10% −5%	+5% +10% +15% +20% +25% +30%	HR	RBI	BA
30	126	.381		1939	31	145	.327
31	133	.352		1940	23	113	.344
30	125	.357		1941	37	120	.406
21	114	.305		1942	36	137	.356
25	95	.290		1946	38	123	.342
20	97	.315		1947	32	114	.343
39	155	.320		1948	25	127	.369
14	67	.346		1949	43	159	.343
32	122	.301		1950	28	97	.317
12	71	.263		1951	30	126	.318

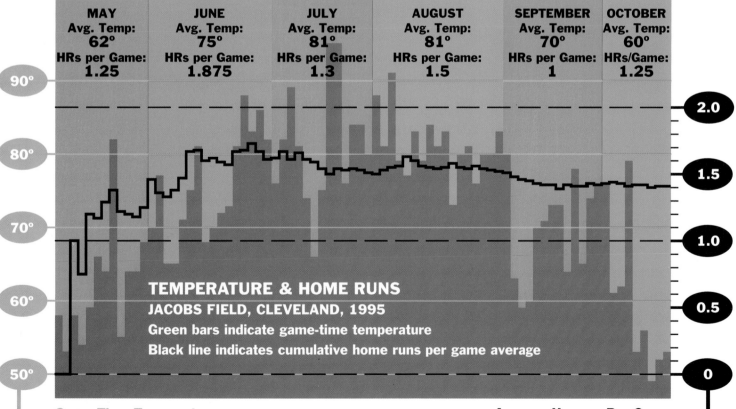

MAY	JUNE	JULY	AUGUST	SEPTEMBER	OCTOBER
Avg. Temp: **62°**	Avg. Temp: **75°**	Avg. Temp: **81°**	Avg. Temp: **81°**	Avg. Temp: **70°**	Avg. Temp: **60°**
HRs per Game: **1.25**	HRs per Game: **1.875**	HRs per Game: **1.3**	HRs per Game: **1.5**	HRs per Game: **1**	HRs/Game: **1.25**

TEMPERATURE & HOME RUNS
JACOBS FIELD, CLEVELAND, 1995
Green bars indicate game-time temperature
Black line indicates cumulative home runs per game average

Game-Time Temperatures

Average Homers Per Game

PHYSICISTS TELL US *that projectiles travel further on hot days, so it stands to reason that the number of home runs hit should climb with the temperature. That can't be stated definitively from this chart of the Cleveland Indians's 1995 season. The Tribe hit 113 dingers at home, in temperatures ranging from 49 to 95 degrees. When the temperature was below 75 degrees Cleveland hit 1.3 homers per game. When it was 75 degrees or hotter, they only hit a few more—1.5 homers per game.*

THE HIGHEST POINT
in the Astrodome is 208 feet, just beyond second base. An 18-story building could fit inside. Mike Schmidt of the Phillies once smashed a shot off the public address speaker that surely would have been a home run anywhere else, but it bounced back down on the field for a single.

Baseball goes Indoors

Texans love baseball as much as anyone, but they hate the oppressive heat, humidity, and mosquitoes that inevitably accompany outdoor games in the summer. In the 1950s, Houston Colt .45 owner Judge Roy Hofheinz worked with geodesic dome inventor Buckminster Fuller on a domed shopping center. When Hofheinz later visited Rome and was told that the Colosseum had been covered with an awning back in 80 A.D., he had a brainstorm: If a dome was good enough for the Romans, it was good enough for the Texans.

The Astrodome (actually Harris County Stadium, and sometimes "the eighth wonder of the world") opened on April 12, 1965. It was the first indoor ballpark, air-conditioned to a comfortable 72 degrees at all times.

No more rain delays. No more wind blowing balls fair, foul, in, or out. No more sun in your eyes. No more steamy July or crisp September. And to fans who feel those things are integral elements of the National Pastime, baseball would never be the same.

Artificial **Turf**

Originally, the Astrodome had natural grass and a clear plastic roof. Unfortunately, the glare was so bad that outfielders started wearing batting helmets to avoid getting beaned by high fly balls. Experiments were conducted with sunglasses and colored baseballs, but neither solved the problem. The roof had to be painted and a replacement solution had to be found for the dead grass.

It just so happened that chemical giant Monsanto had been developing a nylon-and-polyester surface for carpeting. This "ChemGrass" was renamed "AstroTurf" and 125,000 square feet of it (held together by three miles of zippers) was installed in the Astrodome in time for the 1966 season. In the 1970s, many other ballparks would follow suit.

Love it or hate it, there are now more than a thousand playing fields around the world that don't have a blade of grass.

FOUR LAYERS *make up a chunk of AstroTurf. The top layer is one-half inch crinkled nylon fibers. Below that is a foam rubber pad, an asphalt subbase, and a layer of loose gravel.*

The impact of Artificial Turf

In a hundred years, fans build up certain expectations of baseball physics. A ball hit toward a particular part of the field, at a certain angle, with a specific amount of force, should be a single. Or a double. Or whatever.

The same ball hit on an artificial turf field will behave differently. A hard "single" between two outfielders is likely to skip to the wall for a double. A high arcing pop will bounce much higher, forcing outfielders to play more tentatively. They have to be faster runners, but dare fewer diving catches. Conversely, infielders can be more daring on turf, because ground balls are sure to bounce true. The shortstop and third baseman will even intentionally throw to first on a bounce. Batters don't bunt as much, because it's so hard to deaden the ball.

Some fans argue that, like baseball and softball, baseball on grass and on artificial turf are two entirely different games.

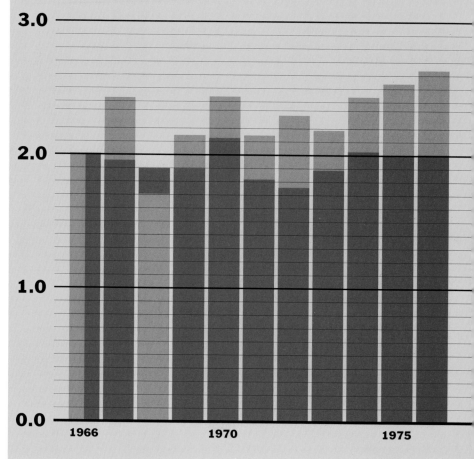

DOUBLES, TRIPLES, AND STEALS

Comparing the average per game totals of doubles, triples and stolen bases between teams that played on artificial surfaces and those that played on natural grass: National League, 1966-1995

3.0

2.0

1.0

0.0

1966   1970   1975

GRASS VS. TURF *There were more doubles, triples, and stolen bases on turf in the National League from 1966 to 1995, according to the chart above. Pete Rose (right) playing first base on the turf at Philadelphia's Veterans Stadium.*

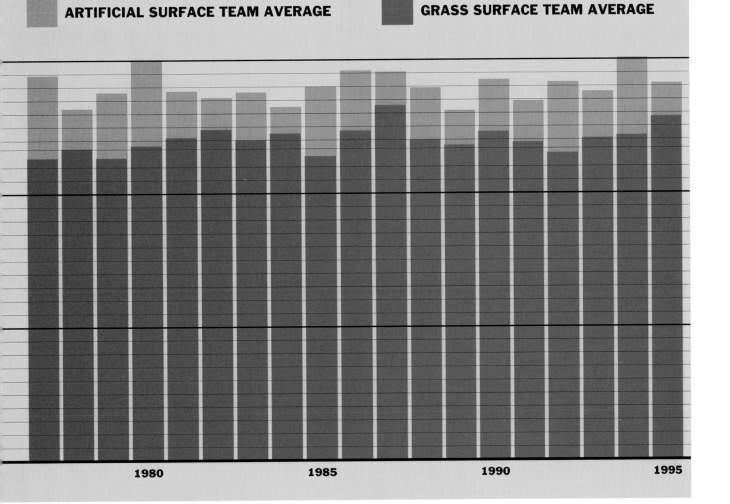

ARTIFICIAL SURFACE TEAM AVERAGE   GRASS SURFACE TEAM AVERAGE

1980   1985   1990   1995

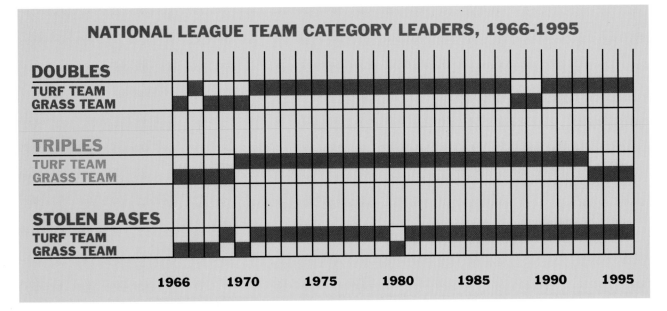

NATIONAL LEAGUE TEAM CATEGORY LEADERS, 1966-1995

DOUBLES
TURF TEAM
GRASS TEAM

TRIPLES
TURF TEAM
GRASS TEAM

STOLEN BASES
TURF TEAM
GRASS TEAM

1966   1970   1975   1980   1985   1990   1995

*"When there is no room for individualism in ballparks,
then there will be no room for individualism in life."*

—Bill Veeck, *in* Veeck, As in Wreck

The era of the
Cookie Cutters

The automobile and the interstate had pretty much conquered America by the 1960s. The Dodgers and Giants had left their crumbling classic ballparks in New York City for the wide open spaces of California. All over the country, people fled the inner cities and moved to newly constructed suburbs. Baseball followed suit.

The stadium designers of the 1970s didn't have to fit their visions into existing city streets. They didn't need to build oddly shaped fields, with weird fences and charming quirks. Instead, they were asked to create "multipurpose facilities" that could host baseball, football, rodeos, rock concerts, and monster truck pulls—with plenty of parking.

The result was a slew of nondescript, nearly identical circular stadiums (no longer called ballparks) that asserted their individuality with the addition of fountains, waterfalls, light shows, and exploding scoreboards. They could seat many more people than the old ballparks, but the seats were farther away from the action. Most of the stadiums had artificial turf.

There was little outcry at the time, but the consensus now is that these stadiums did not provide the ideal conditions for viewing baseball games. While the classic ballparks lasted half a century (and a few are now into their eighties), there is already talk of tearing down and replacing some stadiums built in the 1970s.

DEMOLITION *of Brooklyn's Ebbets Field began on February 23, 1960, breaking the hearts of millions and signaling the end of an era. Four years later the same wrecking ball that destroyed Ebbets was used to bring down another classic New York ballpark—the Polo Grounds (right).*

MULTI-PURPOSE STADIUM *Clockwise from the top left are Riverfront Stadium in Cincinnati, Veterans Stadium in Philadelphia, Busch Stadium in St. Louis, and Three Rivers Stadium in Pittsburgh.*

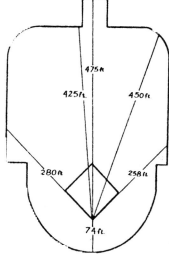

THE POLO GROUNDS *(above) was designed to fit into an existing New York City neighborhood. The Oakland Coliseum (right) had no such restrictions in the suburbs and was built more symmetrically.*

THE BIG ADVANTAGE *of the cookie cutter stadiums was that they were built without columns, which obstructed the view of many fans in older ballparks.*

OPEN AND SHUT CASE *The SkyDome roof (above) consists of four panels made of polyvinylchloride membrane over insulated acoustic steel sheet metal. One panel is fixed, one rotates 180 degrees, and the other two slide straight forward. The roof opens or closes silently in 20 minutes, using up just $8 worth of electricity. It was engineered to work reliably for a hundred years.*

New stadiums:
High Tech

SKYDOME FACTS
At 310 feet, it is the tallest domed stadium. The pitcher's mound is hydraulic and can be raised or lowered at the touch of a button. The $17 million scoreboard is three stories high by nine stories wide. The artificial turf is fastened together by eight miles of zippers. The stadium includes a mall, fitness club, McDonald's, a Hard Rock Cafe, and a luxury hotel with 348 rooms (70 have a view of the field).

One problem with domed stadiums is that you feel like a kid who's been grounded—it's a beautiful day and you're stuck playing indoors. However, the idea of a domed stadium made perfect sense in Toronto, because when the team played its first game at Exhibition Stadium in 1977, the entire field was covered by snow. Toronto broadcaster and former major league catcher Buck Martinez suggested a retractable roof for the new ballpark being built for the Blue Jays on the site of a former water pumping station.

Structural engineer Michael Allen and architect Roderick Robbie spent $700,000 of their own money on prototypes trying to figure out how to make an 11,000-ton roof open and close. Finally, Allen sketched a "telescoping" design on a napkin one day, and the first retractable roofed stadium—SkyDome—was born.

"Several rules of stadium building should be carved on every owner's forehead. Old, if properly refurbished, is always better than new. Smaller is better than bigger. Open is better than closed. Near beats far. Silent visual effects are better than loud ones. Eye pollution hurts attendance. Inside should look as good as outside. Domed stadiums are criminal."

—**Thomas Boswell,** *in* How Life Imitates the World Series

JACOBS FIELD *in Cleveland was designed by the Kansas City architectural firm Hellmuth, Obata, & Kassabaum (HOK), the same folks who gave the world Camden Yards. It is located right in the city, and its design was inspired by Cleveland's steel bridges and Victorian shopping arcades. The left field corner was purposely left open to expose the city skyline. With a little help from players Albert Belle, Carlos Baerga, Kenny Lofton, and Eddie Murray in 1995, Jacobs Field helped propel the Indians to their first pennant in 41 years.*

New stadiums:
Throwbacks

By the time Ebbets, Shibe, Comiskey, and most of the other classic ballparks had been demolished, baseball fans realized those were exactly what they wanted—asymmetrical fields with quirky walls and odd architecture, real grass, and old-fashioned touches that remind us of the good old days.

That's what Baltimore got when Oriole Park at Camden Yards opened in 1992, triggering a second golden age of ballpark design. Camden Yards, nestled right near the harbor and within downtown Baltimore, touched off a wave of rhapsodizing as if a real-life field of dreams had appeared. Architecture critic Paul Goldberger called Camden Yards "a building capable of wiping out in a single gesture 50 years of wretched stadium design."

The success of Camden Yards inspired other cities, and similar "retro" ballparks have gone up in Cleveland, Texas, and Denver.

CAMDEN YARDS *At first, the architects planned to demolish the 94-year-old, 1,016-foot-long B&O warehouse. However, they made it part of the ballpark, and the warehouse has become a landmark like the Green Monster in Fenway and the ivy at Wrigley. The warehouse has Oriole offices, and the windows are a tempting 462 feet from left-handed pull hitters. There is history here. While Camden Yards was being built, archeologists digging in shallow center field unearthed the remnants of the saloon run by Babe Ruth's father from 1906 to 1912.*

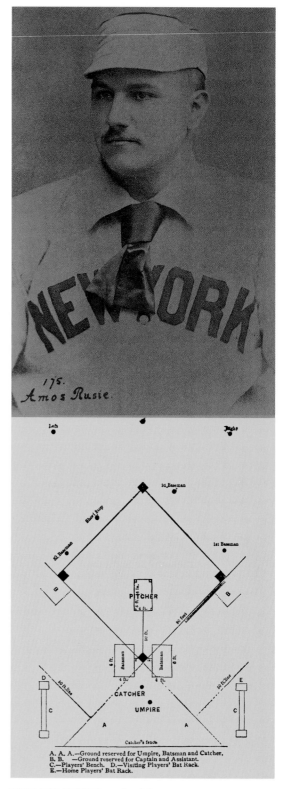

AMOS RUSIE threw so hard, it is said, that he was the reason pitchers were moved from fifty to sixty feet and six inches away from the batter in 1893. "The Hoosier Thunderbolt" had won 98 games in three years before the change. Apparently, the new pitching distance didn't bother Rusie. He won a career high 36 games in 1894.

Ballpark Figures

The story that Abner Doubleday sketched the first baseball diamond with a stick in the dirt of Cooperstown is romantic, but total mythology. If anybody deserves credit for laying out the diamond with the magic "90 feet" between bases, it is Alexander Cartwright (opposite page), a full-time bank teller and part-time leader of the New York Knickerbockers.

In truth, the Cartwright creation story is a myth too. When Cartwright wrote his rules of the game in 1845, he never mentioned anything about 90 feet. He put it this way: "The bases shall be from 'home' to second base, 42 paces; from first to third base, 42 paces, equidistant."

The genius who decided to put four bases exactly 90 feet apart in order to balance the offense and defense has been lost to history. It took baseball about 50 years of experimentation and adjustments in the dimensions to hit on the diamond as we know it today.

THE PITCHER.

UNDERHAND *pitching, with a straight arm was mandatory until pitchers were allowed to bend their elbow in 1878. Sidearm was allowed in 1882 and overhand permitted in 1884. As pitching got faster, the rules were changed to move pitchers back.*

A. A. A.—Ground reserved for Umpire, Batsman and Catcher.
B. B. —Ground reserved for Captain and Assistant.
C.—Players' Bench. D.—Visiting Players' Bat Rack.
E.—Home Players' Bat Rack.

THE DIAMOND *evolved from season to season. Notice the shape of home plate in this 1888 diagram. The plate was at first a circle made of iron. It became a square in 1868, a diamond in 1875, and finally the five-sided shape. The "pitcher's box" was a real box until 1893.*

**ALEXANDER
CARTWRIGHT**
*may not have set the
bases 90 feet apart,
but he did make two
major innovations in
the game. For one, he
decided that each side
would be retired after
three outs. Secondly,
he had the defense
put runners out by
throwing the ball to a
fielder covering a
base. Before this, the
defense had to hit the
runner with the ball,
which was called
"soaking."*

**YOU COULD
LOOK IT UP** *This*
Base Ball Player's
Pocket Companion
*helped clarify the
rules confusion for
the athlete of 1859.*

ALL FOUL LINES *are not created equal. If the paint is applied very thickly, a rolling bunt will tend to bump off the line and stay in fair territory. If a visiting team has superior bunters, some groundskeepers will tilt the lines the other way to make bunts roll foul. The lines at Fenway Park are painted (right).*

MARSHALL BOSSARD *was a member of the legendary Bossard family, groundskeepers from 1936 to today. They became famous for virtually sculpting the field at Cleveland Stadium to fit the strengths and weaknesses of the Indians.*

Diamond
Doctoring

Home field advantage means more than just getting the crowd on your side. Subtle manipulation of the playing field can neutralize a team's advantages and disadvantages. A savvy groundskeeper will study his team and the visiting teams to see what he can do to make the playing field a little less level, so to speak.

If the home team has a great sinker baller, the groundskeeper will let the grass grow a little higher to absorb grounders. If they have a big power pitcher, he might build the pitcher's mound a little higher to make the guy seem more imposing. And just to throw off the visitors, he'll make the mound in their bullpen a different height than the one on the field. For the most part, groundskeeping tricks are perfectly legal. When the groundskeeper starts moving the fences in and out between innings, well, that's a different story.

WATER *has a funny way of influencing a baseball game. If the base paths are soaked, stolen base specialists can't get a good jump. If the infield grass is drenched, grounders slow down for sluggish infielders. If the area in front of the plate is wet, bunts will die there. This strategy was used in Detroit during Ty Cobb's day, and that area came to be known as "Cobb's Lake."*

EDDIE STANKY *managed the White Sox in the 1960s and was known for monkeying with the mound, foul lines, and the height of the grass. When a power-hitting team like the Yankees came to town, Stanky allegedly put the baseballs in a freezer to deaden them.*

TARP TRICKS *The Cleveland Indians used to have two tarps. One could be rolled out in two minutes, the other took 20 minutes. If the Indians were leading when a downpour occurred, out came the "fast" tarp. If the "Tribe" was behind, they'd roll out the slow tarp and hope the umps called a rainout.*

MICKEY MANTLE *got a foot caught in an exposed drainpipe during the 1951 World Series at Yankee Stadium (above). The rookie, who was once clocked at 3.1 seconds from home to first, would consequently suffer painful knee and leg problems for the next 17 years of his Hall of Fame career.*

PARK IT *The Astrodome (above left) actually had one rainout—it rained so much, the fans couldn't get there. Getting fans to the ballpark has always been the driving force in determining where ballparks are built. It's the reason New York City once had three teams, and the reason why two of them moved to California in the late 1950s. Baseball has expanded into Canada, and major league teams will probably appear in other countries. The Toronto Blue Jays played in Exhibition Stadium (above right) before the SkyDome was built.*

One last look

Around the Park

GEHRIG'S LOCKER *Today's clubhouse looks more like an upscale health club than a dingy locker room.*

The true fan doesn't just get up and leave the ballpark when the final out in the ninth inning is made. He sits in his seat for a few minutes going over his scorecard, relaxing, and watching the crowd file out. Finally, when the stadium is nearly empty and the ushers start giving him the evil eye, he stands, stretches, and goes over to the railing. The groundskeepers are tending the field. The security men ring the foul lines, trying to appear intimidating. The true fan takes in the huge expanse of green, sighs, and walks away, turning around one last time to watch the last sliver of green disappear, until next time.

As the philosopher Yogi Berra may—or may not—have said, "It ain't over till it's over." And even then, it still ain't over.

SCOREBOARDS *have gone from manual (left top, the operator inside Yankee Stadium's board) to mechanical (left middle, Yankee Stadium in the 1940s) to electronic (left bottom, Cincinnati's Riverfront Stadium announcing the hit that made Pete Rose the all-time hit leader.)*

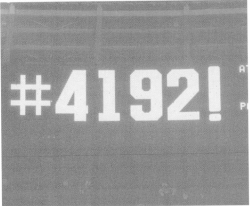

BILLBOARDS *on highways are considered to be visual pollution, but in ballparks they somehow add a warm element and remind fans of simpler times. The pennant (above) is raised over the Polo Grounds at the start of the 1918 season. The most famous ballpark ad was the yellow "Hit Sign, Win Suit" billboard at Ebbets Field. Clothier Abe Stark didn't have to give away many suits, thanks to the fielding of the Dodger right fielder Carl Furillo.*

ONE OF THE FEW PLACES *in the world where it is socially acceptable to toss your garbage on the ground is at the ballpark.*

LITTLE LEAGUE BASEBALL • A BASEBALL EDUCATION

SCOUTING • THE MINOR LEAGUES • BASEBALL'S

HEIRARCHY • TRADES • STATISTICS • SPRING

TRAINING • THE CEREMONY OF THE GAME • ROAD

TRIPS, INJURIES & OTHER BAT–AND–BALL GAMES

Chapter Five

Everybody longs for the good old days. They always have, and they always will. Over 150 seasons, baseball has developed a structure that is familiar yet still evolving. The season begins with the buds of spring and ends when the trees shed their leaves. From Little League all the way to the Hall of Fame, players are funneled through the system. Young phenoms arrive like shooting stars and usually fizzle out just as quickly. New teams are born, and they're always lousy. Commissioners come and go. With every new decade, Minnie Minoso makes a comeback. Then somebody throws out the first ball, everybody stands up in the middle of the seventh, and it ain't over till it's over. And when it's over, everybody argues about what happened until spring training arrives.

Clockwise across spread, from top left: a Little Leaguer in action; Elias Baseball Analyst Abstract; President Wilson throws out the first ball; Ted Williams instructs the troops; Paul and Dizzy Dean; Abner Doubleday; and 19th century magnates.

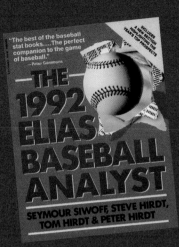

The Structure of Baseball

The making of a Baseball Player

NOT SO LITTLE LEAGUE *Since its inception in 1939, Little League has grown from three teams to 196,000. Clarence Brumm (above) of Colton, California, blows a bubble during a play in the 1954 Little League World Series in Williamsport, Pennsylvania.*

"**A** boy cannot begin playing ball too early," wrote Christy Mathewson. "I might almost say that while he's still creeping on all fours, he should have a rubber bouncing ball." That advice has been taken to heart by generations of hopeful Dads who have littered the nursery with bat, ball, and glove. And after seven or so seasons of backyard catch and T–ball, our phenom in waiting is ready for the big time: Little League. As one of more than three million players in 91 countries, he (and she) will learn, as the organization's manifesto reminds us, the rewards of teamwork, the responsibility of membership, respect for authority, and how to win and lose with dignity. As for Dad, the season's likely to be a little more stressful. "For the parent of a Little Leaguer," former major league pitcher Earl Wilson points out, "a baseball game is simply a nervous breakdown divided into innings."

CAMPING IT UP *Youngsters, like this group at the 1968 Ted Williams Baseball Camp, have long spent their summers learning the finer points of the double play, and in recent years adult fantasy campers have joined in the fun.*

ME AN' PAUL *When Paul Dean joined the St. Louis Cardinals staff in 1934, his brother Dizzy boasted that the pair would win between 45 and 50 games. "How many will you win, Diz?" asked a reporter. "Why, all the games that Paul don't." Paul won 19, Dizzy pitched in with 30 and they led the Gashouse Gang to a World Series victory.*

Is it the **Genes?**

Are major leaguers born or are they made? Biological determinists would note that any short list of the best players in the game has to include Barry Bonds, Ken Griffey Jr., Moises Alou, and Roberto Alomar, all the sons of former major leaguers. Behaviorists would counter that it was environment (i.e., hanging around a major league clubhouse) that gave these guys a leg up. But whether it's nature or nurture (or

some combination of the two), one thing's for sure: the ingredients for big-league success are parceled out unequally within families. The home run record for brothers is 768, held by the Aarons: Hank hit 755; Tommie hit 13.

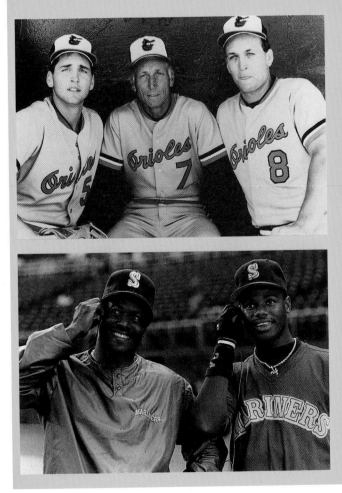

GENERATIONS *Ray Boone, shortstop for the Indians and Tigers, gets stuck up by his son Bob (above). Bob would put in 19 years as a big-league catcher and for a time held the career record for most games caught. His son Bret is now a major league second baseman and the first third-generation big leaguer. The Ripkens (left, top)—Billy, Cal Sr., and Cal Jr.: Dad managed both his sons in 1988. Ken Griffey Sr. (left, bottom) stuck around long enough to play with Ken Griffey Jr. in Seattle, and on September 14, 1990, they hit back-to-back homers.*

COLLEGE WORLD SERIES *BYU shortstop Mike Staffieri is upended by Harvard centerfielder Dave Ignacio in the 1971 College World Series in Omaha.*

HALL OF FAMER *Reggie Jackson was just one of the future big leaguers to play for perennial power Arizona State. Other ASU baseball alumni include Rick Monday, Sal Bando, Bob Horner, Floyd Bannister, Hubie Brooks, Mike Devereaux, Pat Listach, and former Dallas Cowboy quarterback Danny White.*

"I don't care how many of them college degrees you got. They ain't learned you to hit that curveball no better than me."

—Buck Crouse,

White Sox catcher, to Princeton grad Moe Berg

Higher **Education**

1988 CHAMPS *Lewis and Clark State College Warriors celebrate after winning the 1988 National Association of Intercollegiate Athletics Championships.*

Baseball and schooling have always gone together like reading, writing, and running the bases. The first college match was played between Amherst and Williams on July 1, 1859 (Amherst won 73-32), and seven years later the young ladies of Vassar took up the game. However, the game's pragmatism wasn't always well received in the ivory towers. "I understand that a curve ball is thrown with a deliberate attempt to deceive. Surely that is an ability we should not want to foster at Harvard," said president Charles William Eliot.

These days, both high school squads and college teams attract scouts by the dozens and are prime proving grounds for legitimate future major leaguers—It's called vocational training.

MEL OTT (*inset left*) *went from high school to the Hall of Fame with only one stop in between—a 22-year stint with the New York Giants.*

Scouts

Beating the Bushes

"**A**gainst Santa Clara University he was hit hard by players I did not grade as hitters. From his performance in this game, I could not consider him a prospect." Care to guess the subject of this 1965 scouting report? Would you believe Tom Seaver? Mistakes like this show what an inexact science it is to project how a high school shortstop will fare against Randy Johnson, or whether a pitcher will add five mph to his fastball. But since there isn't a better way, major league scout watch thousands of high school and college games every season in search of the next Tom Seaver—and hope they don't catch him on a bad day.

BONUS BABIES *Dodger scouting director Al Campanis (above, center) smiles as brothers Joe (above, left) and Gary Moeller (above, right) sign contracts that include bonuses totaling $75,000. Joe, 17, had posted an exceptional 0.44 high school ERA, and pitched for the Dodgers for eight years between 1962 and 1971. Gary had hit .480 as a catcher, but never made it to the majors.*

HERE, THERE, AND EVERYWHERE *Scouts often travel in packs, flocking to where the prospects are. Forty-five big-league scouts (above) sized up 300 players at the 1962 Johnstown, Pennsylvania, Amateur Baseball Association Tournament. Two dozen scouts (opposite) showed up at the American Legion Little World Series in Bismarck, North Dakota, that same year.*

IT'S A GAMBLE *Jack Dunn and Ned Hanlon look on as the Boston Red Sox gamble on a relatively unknown pitcher named Babe Ruth, here signing his first big-league contract in 1914.*

"They can play music all they want. They can run dancing elephants out there. But don't play between pitches. There's got to be some professionalism."

—Lee Elia, *Clearwater Phillies manager,*

after pulling his team off the field to protest the playing of polka music

Not so bush:

The Minor Leagues

There are two faces to minor league baseball. On the one hand, there's a tousled, romantic Bull Durham quality to the game—quaint old stadiums, cheesy mascots, and tickets so cheap you can afford not to pay attention. And there's the scent of hope in the air, as wide-eyed farmhands try to avoid becoming

NO THANKS *Another player to skip the minors altogether was Ernie Banks, who went straight from the Negro Leagues to the Chicago Cubs in 1953.*

never-wases, and former big leaguers forestall the advent of has-been-dom. The lure of The Show is why they keep riding the buses. But there's the rub. Minor league baseball is just about the only game where there's a downside to winning. There's nothing that attracts the attention of the big club like success, and, Eastern League pennant race or not, it's off to the big leagues for your best players. So if your shortstop is tearing up the league, next week you could be watching him on television.

BIG IDEAS *are useful when you don't have big names to lure fans to the park. Minor league impressario Joe Enge (above) entertains a pachyderm as part of a promotion.*

MORE THAN MINOR *The Baltimore Orioles of 1914 (left) featured a happy fat kid, far right, named Babe Ruth. Lefty Grove was another future Hall of Famer who toiled for owner Jack Dunn. Before the advent of the farm system, minor league teams owned the rights to their players and made money by selling their stars to major league clubs.*

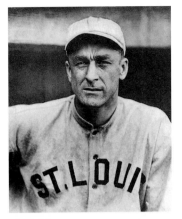

BUYING THE FARM *In the early 1920s, Cardinal GM Branch Rickey (left) reasoned that he could skirt escalating player costs by signing hundreds of young prospects and developing them through a farm system of interconnected teams from the low minors on up. Largely stocked by young men left otherwise jobless by the Depression, Rickey's system grew to 33 teams by 1937. His quality-through-quantity plan produced immediate results—the Cards won the World Series in 1926 with a squad that included home-grown Hall of Famers Chick Hafey and Jim Bottomley—and was soon widely imitated by other major league clubs.*

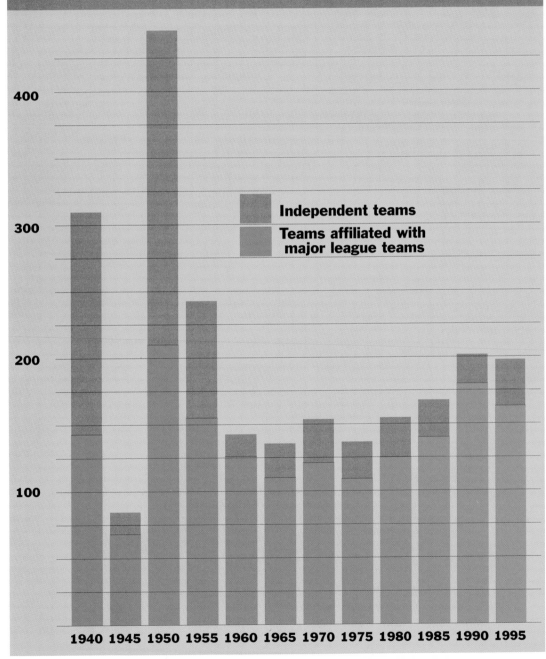

NUMBER OF MINOR LEAGUE TEAMS, 1940-1995

- 400
- 300
- 200
- 100

Independent teams
Teams affiliated with major league teams

1940 1945 1950 1955 1960 1965 1970 1975 1980 1985 1990 1995

MINOR RESURGENCE

The number of minor league teams peaked in 1950 at 446. Within the next 15 years, with televised major league games cutting into minor league attendance, and the rise of college baseball and the advent of the entry draft diminishing the role of the minor leagues' in player development, that number dropped to only 136. Since the mid '60s, the trend has reversed itself. By the late '80s, teams like the Buffalo Bisons were drawing over a million fans annually and the cost of major league franchises spiraled out of the reach of all but the super-wealthy, prompting wannabe baseball barons to pay millions for minor league clubs that could have been had for just the back debts a little more than a decade before.

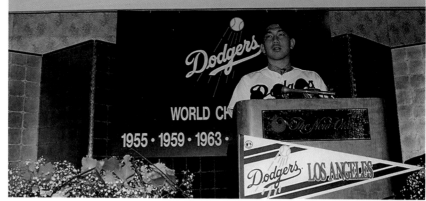

HIDEO NOMO *went 78-46 for the Kintetsu Buffaloes of the Japanese Pacific League before coming to Los Angeles in 1995 and becoming the fourth consecutive Dodger to win the Jackie Robinson Award as NL Rookie of the Year.*

FRANK ROBINSON *won the NL Rookie of the Year award in 1956, hitting 38 home runs (a rookie record at that time). He went on to win MVP awards in both leagues, before becoming baseball's first black manager.*

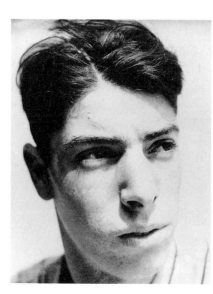

Razzing the **Rookies**

It's not easy being a rookie. The veterans steal your clothes while you're in the shower and replace them with a clashing plaid ensemble that would be Mr. Blackwell's worst nightmare. And the manager is always eyeing you suspiciously, just looking for an excuse to sit you on the bench and go back to Plan A. It's enough to make you want to go back to the minors. Almost. Yet a few rookies rise above the adversity, and glide right into great things: 30 homers, 18 wins, a bushelful of saves. But even before the Rookie of the Year trophy can collect any dust, the whispers begin again. Can you say sophomore slump?

GARY MATTHEWS'S FIVE RULES FOR ROOKIES

1. No high fives until the late innings.

2. Play to win, but play clean.

3. Say what you mean, but pick your spots.

4. Put personal problems aside when you play the game.

5. Respect and friendship are the keys.

JOE DIMAGGIO *went straight from being a minor league star in his hometown of San Francisco, where he compiled a 61-game hitting streak in 1933, to being a big-league star with the Yankees, where he hit .323 with 125 RBIs in 1936. Still he didn't completely bypass rookie culture shock: "I can remember a reporter asking for a quote . . . I thought it was some kind of a soft drink."*

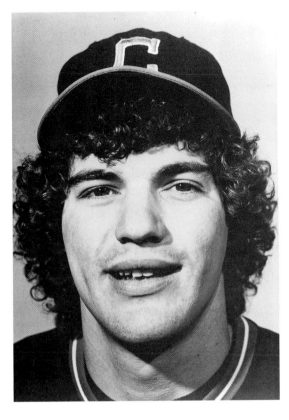

> "*A ball player's got to be kept hungry to become a big-leaguer. That's why no boy from a rich family ever made it in the big leagues.*"
>
> ## —Joe DiMaggio

FLASHES IN THE PAN *A Rookie of the Year award doesn't guarantee a long and successful career. Joe Charboneau (above, left), the eccentric Cleveland outfielder who opened beer bottles with his eye sockets, found himself back in the minors only a year after winning the 1980 Rookie of the Year award. He had only 194 more big-league at bats before his career was over. The AL's top rookie in 1976, Mark Fidrych (above, right) went 19-9 for the Tigers while captivating fans by talking to the ball and getting down on his hands and knees to manicure the mound. He came down with knee and arm problems the next year and won only 10 more games before retiring in 1980. The 1976 NL Rookie of the Year Butch Metzger (left) went 11-4 with a 2.92 ERA for the Padres. He would go 9-7 the rest of his career.*

FERNANDOMANIA *In 1981, Dodger rookie Fernando Valenzuela (right) brightened a strike-marred season by pitching eight shutouts, winning the NL Rookie of the Year award and the Cy Young Award, and helping Los Angeles to the World Championship.*

THE COMMISSIONER'S OFFICE *was first filled by Judge Kenesaw Mountain Landis, who had earlier ruled in baseball's favor in an antitrust case brought by the Federal League. Before signing on, Landis stipulated that he would have the job for life and wouldn't be criticized publicly by the owners.*

Baseball's
Hierarchy

Just as the president is sworn to uphold the Constitution, baseball's commissioner has his own rite of allegiance, to the best interests of the game. He is the game's moral compass. Betting on baseball? You're outta here. Hanging out with gamblers? Well, don't let it happen again. Violating the drug policy? Hit the showers. And that allegiance supersedes considerations of due process and even good sense—the Black Sox players suspended by Judge Landis were acquitted in court, while Ford Frick put an asterisk next to Roger Maris's 61 homers in a nonexistant record book. This kind of absolute power is not without its appeal; Bart Giamatti decided he'd rather run baseball than run Yale. But inevitably, the commissioner's role as baseball's Solomon puts him at odds with the very people who employ him, the owners. So from Landis's unpopular stand against the farm system to Fay Vincent's refusal to take a hard line on labor, every commissioner has created controversy. It's a tough job, and maybe, like the presidency, one best left to someone else. "I'd rather be an attendant in a gas station. You wipe a windshield and they say, 'thank you.'" says Padres president Buzzie Bavasi. "Nobody every says thank you to the commissioner of baseball."

WILLIAM HULBERT *founded the National League in 1876, and was responsible for centralizing control of the game by enforcing schedules, establishing geographical territories, and stamping out gambling and crooked play. He also devised the reserve clause which effectively bound players to their teams in perpetuity.*

THE PLAYERS LEAGUE *of 1890, the brainchild of John Montgomery Ward (right) arose from player dissatisfaction with the reserve clause and the owners' proposed $2,500 salary cap. The league attracted stars like King Kelly, but financial problems caused it to fold after one season.*

COMMISSIONERS PAST *Bowie Kuhn, William Eckert, Ford Frick, and Happy Chandler (above, left to right) ruled the game for almost four decades. Chandler took office two years before Jackie Robinson broke the color barrier, while Kuhn's reign saw the first million-dollar-a-year ballplayer.*

THE AMERICAN LEAGUE *under President Ban Johnson (right) lured players like Nap Lajoie, Cy Young, and Big Ed Delahanty from the National League in 1901 and 1902. In 1903 a truce was declared and the AL (a minor league circuit once known as the Western League) became the second major league.*

THE LEAGUE PRESIDENTS *lend their signatures to official baseballs (left), rule on appeals, oversee umpires, and hand out suspensions. Above all, they must maintain the appearance of impartiality. Announcer Hank Greenwald observed, "The president of the league is the only guy who comes to the ballgame and roots for the umpires."*

Pete Gray serves as an icon of wartime baseball.

LANDIS, a former federal judge, was given a free hand to clean up the sport. He not only suspended for life eight White Sox players accused of throwing the 1919 World Series (including Lefty Williams, below), but also went so far as to ban pitcher Dickie Kerr for pitching in an exhibition against some of the outcast Sox. In another controversial decision, he bestowed free agency upon 74 Cardinal farmhands and 91 Detroit minor leaguers, citing "secret understandings" between the teams and the farm club owners.

FRICK presided over the first franchise shuffling since 1903: the Braves moved from Boston to Milwaukee, the A's from Philadelphia to Kansas City, the Browns from St. Louis to Baltimore, the Giants from New York to San Francisco, and the Dodgers from Brooklyn to Los Angeles. He also oversaw the expansion of teams into Los Angeles, Washington, New York, and Houston. Frick was best known for attaching a symbolic asterisk to Roger Maris's 1961 home run record.

| KENESAW LANDIS 1920–1944 | HAPPY CHANDLER 1945–51 | FORD FRICK 1951–1965 | WILLIAM ECKERT 1965–1968 |

CHANDLER saw Jackie Robinson break the color barrier during his term, but is best known for his suspension of Robinson's manager, Leo Durocher (below) on gambling charges. He also blacklisted 18 players who had jumped to the Mexican League, including Sal Maglie, but quietly reinstated them when Giant farmhand Danny Gardella brought suit. Chandler's gambling probe of Yankee owner Dell Webb may have proven to be his downfall, and the commissioner wasn't offered a contract extension.

ECKERT'S brief term set the stage for player/owner confrontations that would take place under Bowie Kuhn. He angered owners by siding with Roberto Clemente (below), Maury Wills, Rusty Staub, and others who chose not to play in spring training games after the assassination of Martin Luther King. On the labor front, Marvin Miller became the head of the Players Association in 1966, and Eckert was ousted in midterm amid signs of an impending players' strike.

Commissioners

KUHN *was commissioner during a period of great labor unrest. He watched as Miller called baseball's first players' strike in 1969, and saw the scenario repeated in 1972 and 1981. The Dave McNally/Andy Messersmith arbitration decision awarded players free agency in 1977, leading to higher salaries. Kuhn also suspended George Steinbrenner for making illegal contibutions to the Nixon campaign, nullified Charlie Finley's cash sales of Joe Rudi and Rollie Fingers to the Red Sox and Vida Blue to the Yankees, and publicly denounced Jim Bouton's taboo-breaking book, Ball Four.*

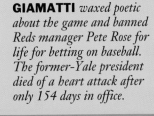

GIAMATTI *waxed poetic about the game and banned Reds manager Pete Rose for life for betting on baseball. The former-Yale president died of a heart attack after only 154 days in office.*

| **BOWIE KUHN** 1968–1984 | **PETER UEBERROTH** 1984–1989 | **BART GIAMATTI** 1989 | **FAY VINCENT** 1989–1993 |

UEBERROTH, *former head of the Los Angeles Olympic Organizing Committee, signed lucrative TV deals with CBS and ESPN. Baseball's drug problem came to light during his term, and he handed down suspensions to Steve Howe, Pascual Perez, and others.*

VINCENT, *Giamatti's deputy commissioner, presided over the quake-marred 1989 World Series. He suspended Yankee owner George Steinbrenner for enlisting the aid of felon Howie Spira to smear Dave Winfield. His permanent drug-related suspension of Steve Howe was overturned. His move to realign the NL met with resistance from the powerful Chicago Cubs, and after the owners attempted to strip him of his labor-relations authority and sent him a message in the form of a no-confidence vote, Vincent resigned, citing "the best interests of baseball." He was replaced by interim commissioner, Milwaukee Brewers owner Bud Selig.*

Curt Flood: an early fighter in the free-agency wars

HOT TICKETS
Every team's goal is to be printing World Series tickets in October, like the ones (above) from Crosley Field in Cincinnati in 1939.

The art of
Building a Winner

There's no one way to build a winner. Pick a tactic, and there's been a time that it *has* worked. Free agent frenzy? The Yankees of the late '70s cherry picked the market—and won. Bargain basement build-up? The 1991 Twins went from worst to first with Kirby Puckett and a lot of guys you never heard of—until October. Rent a player? The Toronto Blue Jays added David Cone in mid-season of 1993, and Rickey Henderson in mid-course the following year. The end result was back to back world titles. Rebuilding through the farm system? You need look no further than the 1995 Atlanta Braves, laden with farm prospects like Tom Glavine, Steve Avery, Dave Justice, and Chipper Jones. The moral of the story is that it doesn't matter which route you choose, as long as you keep moving forward.

DYNASTY *In their history the Yankees have won 33 pennants, and their greatest period of American League dominance came between 1949 and 1964. Over that 16-year span, the Bombers, led first by Joe DiMaggio and later by Mickey Mantle, failed to earn a trip to the Fall Classic only twice, and won nine World Series titles, including five in a row between 1949 and 1953. World Series rings (below) are of various vintages.*

Year	Record	Finish

1983   89-73   4th, 9 games behind Baltimore
Dramatic improvement; their first winning season. Key additions: George Bell, a free-agent signing in 1978, and Tony Fernandez, signed as a 16-year old in 1979.

1984   89-73   2nd, 15 games behind Detroit
The Tigers start out 35-5 and run away with the division. **3B Kelly Gruber** *obtained in the Rule V. draft from Cleveland.* **P Jimmy Key** *debuts; he was a 3rd round draft choice in 1982.*

1985   99-62   1st, 2 games ahead of New York
A Division Championship: but in the LCS, they blow a 3-1 game advantage to KC and lose three straight. **SS Manny Lee,** *another Rule V draft acquisition, Dec. 3 1984, from Astros.* **P Tom Henke** *drafted from Texas in the player compensation pool draft, Jan 24, 1985; pick received for Rangers signing of Cliff Johnson Dec. 5, 1984.*

1986   86-76   4th, 9.5 games behind Boston
P Duane Ward *obtained from Atlanta for pitcher Doyle Alexander, July 6 1986 (Doyle would return to haunt the Jays). Fred McGriff acquired in a five-man deal with the Yankees, debuts Dec. 9, 1982.*

1987   96-66   2nd, 2 games behind Detroit
They lose their last seven games to blow the Division Championship Doyle Alexander, an August acquisition, goes 9-0 for Detroit. **P David Wells,** *their second round pick in the 1982 draft and minor-league* **P Juan Guzman** *acquired from Los Angeles for Mike Sharperson debuts in a late-season deal*

1988   87-75   3rd, 2 games behind Boston
P Todd Stottlemyre *debuts; he was a 1985 secondary-phase draft choice. Another 1982 draftee,* **C Pat Borders,** *debuts.*

1989   89-73   1st, 2 games ahead of Milwaukee
But Oakland rolls over them in the LCS. **1B John Olerud** *is selected in the third round of the free agent draft and joins the team directly from Washington State University.*

1990   86-76   2nd, 2 games behind Boston
Key additions: Mark Whiten, Luis Sojo. One who got away: Former Jay Cecil Fielder, who hit 51 homers for Detroit, by way of Japan.

1991   91-71   1st, 7 games ahead of Det. and Bos.
Blockbuster offseason trade: Tony Fernandez and Fred McGriff to SD for **OF Joe Carter** *and* **2B Roberto Alomar;** **CF Devon White** *is signed as a free agent;* **P Pat Hentgen** *arrives, from the 1986 draft. The Twins beat them 4-1 in LCS.*

1992   96-66   1st, 4 games ahead of Milwaukee
Free agent signings: **DH Dave Winfield** *and* **P Jack Morris** **P David Cone** *picked up in August. Winfield's double in the tenth inning of WS game six wins the title for Toronto*

1993   95-67   1st, 7 games ahead of New York
P Dave Stewart *and* **DH Paul Molitor** *signed.* **OF Rickey Henderson** *the rented gun. Carter's HR in game six gives the Jays another crown.*

Players in red were key members of one or both championship teams.

Joe Carter

Toronto's road to a **Title**

In 1977, the Toronto Blue Jays entered the strong American League East. And in their first six years they finished last. But management took a long-term view by choosing to build a strong farm system, scouting aggressively in Latin America, and taking advantage of baseball's arcane Rule V draft rules. By 1985, the patience began to pay off and the Jays won their first AL East title. By adding free agents they went on to win world titles in 1992 and 1993.

"I went through life as 'the player to be named later.'"

—Joe Garagiola

A timeline of
Trades

Grass is always greener on the other side. Ther''s something about the unknown that's irresistible. Which is why a general manager looks at his own lineup and sees nothing but an array of liabilities. And across the diamond, he sees nothing but potential. The phone rings. "Sow's ear for a silk purse? You've got a deal." But, of course, the guy on the other end of the line is thinking the same thing. So a smart GM keeps these words of wisdom from Bill Veeck in plain sight: Sometimes the best deals are the ones you *don't* make.

YANKEE BENEFACTOR *Boston Red Sox owner Harry Frazee (below) not only sold budding star Babe Ruth (left) to the Yankees in 1920 so he could pay his club's creditors and finance his play,* No, No Nannette, *in other deals he also shipped pitchers Waite Hoyt, Herb Pennock, Sam Jones, Joe Bush; catcher Wally Schang; and infielders Everett Scott and Joe Dugan to the Bronx. This talent shift resulted in six Yankee pennants during the decade and nine last-place finishes for the Red Sox.*

TWO HALL OF FAMERS *were involved in one of the most lopsided trades of all time in 1900. The Reds got veteran pitcher Amos Rusie, who had won 245 games and didn't have a single victory left in his arm, while the Giants acquired young hurler Christy Mathewson (below), who would go on to notch 372 victories for New York.*

BOBO NEWSOM *was traded 10 times between 1935 and 1947. Seven of those times he was traded either from or to the Washington Senators.*

1900   1910   1920   1930

PAYBACK TIME *In 1916, the Giants traded Mathewson and outfielder Edd Roush to Cincinnati for Buck Herzog and Wade Killefer. Mathewson won only one game for the Reds, but Roush became a .325 lifetime hitter and, eventually, a Hall of Famer.*

BREAKING UP THAT OLD GANG
Rather than pay the salaries necessary to keep his players from jumping to rival Federal League, A's owner Connie

Mack broke up a team that won five pennants and three World Series in six years. He sold Eddie Collins for $50,000 and released Jack Coombs, Eddie Plank, and Chief Bender. Mack slowly rebuilt the club, winning back-to-back championships in 1929 and 1930, but the Depression forced him to repeat the sell-off in 1932, selling off future Hall of Famers Jimmie Foxx (inset), Lefty Grove, Al Simmons, and Mickey Cochrane. The team finished last nine times between 1935 and 1946.

FRANK "TRADER" LANE *was vilified by Cleveland fans when in 1960 he traded local hero and home run champ Rocky Colavito to Detroit for batting champion Harvey Kuenn (left). Lane announced, "I traded a hamburger for a steak." Kuenn was gone in a year, while Colavito hit 45 homers for the Tigers. In 1962 when talks became intricate, Lane and the Tigers decided to swap managers—Joe Gordon for Jimmy Dykes—rather than exchange players.*

LOU BROCK *was a 25-year-old .250 hitting outfielder for the Cubs. After being traded to the Cardinals in 1964, Brock entered the Hall of Fame portion of his career, collecting a total of 3,023 hits, stealing a career record 938 bases, and earning election to Cooperstown in 1985.*

RED SCHOENDIENST *was traded from the New York Giants to the Milwaukee Braves in mid-season despite leading the NL with 200 hits in 1957.*

1940   **1950**   **1960**   **1970**   **1980**   **1990**

A THREE-WAY DEAL *between Chicago White Sox, Cleveland Indians, and Philadelphia A's in April 1951 caused the league's eventual homer and RBI champion, Gus Zernial to switch from the White Sox to the A's. Minnie Minoso moved from the Indians to the White Sox and led the league in triples and steals.*

TRADING AWAY A TRIPLE CROWN *Cincinnati tired of long-time star Frank Robinson. Baltimore offered pitcher Milt Pappas. Cincy finished 7th, while Robinson collected an MVP award and a world series ring for the 1966 Orioles*

YOUTH FOR EXPERIENCE *was the theme of a 1987 late-season deal between the Tigers and the Atlanta Braves. Detroit acquired veteran pitcher Doyle Alexander for a minor leaguer. Alexander would go 9-0 for the Tigers, helping them clinch the AL East. The minor leaguer Atlanta picked up was John Smoltz, who has become a three-time All-Star for the Braves.*

THE BIGGEST DEAL *in baseball history was an 18-player trade between the New York Yankees and the Baltimore Orioles completed on December 1, 1954. The Orioles got Gene Woodling, Willie Miranda, Gus Triandos, and Hal Smith, while the Yankees acquired hurlers Bob Turley and Don Larsen, who would go on to pitch a perfect game in the 1956 World Series.*

THE METS, *looking to solve a long-standing problem at third base, acquired Jim Fregosi from the California Angels, for a wild, young right-hander named Nolan Ryan (left). By the time Ryan retired in 1993 with 324 wins and 5,714 strikeouts, Fregosi, who played only 146 games for the Mets, had been retired as a player for 15 years and was in his tenth season as a manager.*

ROGER MARIS *in 1961 began losing his hair from the strain of chasing Babe Ruth's single-season home run record. Maris tied the record in his 684th plate appearance, five fewer than Ruth needed.*

Lies, damned lies, and Statistics

Try and imagine baseball without statistics. There would be no .300 hitters. No 20-game winners. No 30/30 Club. Not even a Mendoza Line. Statistics not only help us keep track of who's tearing it up and who's stinking it up, they shape the way we think about the game. They provide us with bizarre and revealing trivia. (Did you know that Roger Maris didn't draw one intentional walk the year he hit 61 homers with Mickey Mantle hitting behind him?) Numbers tell stories all by themselves (56, 61, 755, and 4,256 to name four). They even affect the way the game is played. (Did you ever notice how free swingers suddenly become Wade Boggs wanna-bes when they get within a few whiffs of the single-season strikeout record?) Was Jim Bouton right when he said that statistics are as interesting as a first base coach? Only if the first base coach is Casey Stengel.

THE SOCIETY FOR AMERICAN BASE-BALL RESEARCH *can take credit in the 1970s and '80s for bringing baseball stats out of the dark ages. Sabremetricians like Bill James, Pete Palmer, and John Thorn have made strong arguments, for example, that an on-base percentage is more important than batting average, ERA is a more reliable yardstick than win-loss record, and a high fielding percentage doesn't necessarily correspond to defensive excellence. While some of their more arcane stats, like runs produced and linear weights, remain the province of serious students of the game, other innovations, like situational breakdowns, have gone mainstream and are even used by major league managers.*

RED HOT *Joe Morgan (above) not only put up great numbers (.395 on base percentage, eight seasons with 100 or more runs scored, 80 per cent stolen base rate), he also kept track of every at bat and every pitcher he faced. Player statistics are also used by player agents and general managers to justify their positions during salary arbitrations.*

A statistics **Timeline**

It may have always been a part of the game, but it's not a statistic until somebody counts it. Below is a list of familiar statistics, when they were first officially compiled, and who were the first league leaders.

Joe McGinnity

BATTING AVERAGE
1877 NL Deacon White, Boston Red Sox **.387**

INNINGS PITCHED
1903 NL Joe McGinnity, New York Giants **434**
1908 AL Ed Walsh, Chicago White Sox **464**

COMPLETE GAMES
1910 NL Wilbur Cooper, Pittsburgh Pirates **27**
1922 AL Walter Johnson, Washington Senators **38**

ERA
1912 NL Jeff Tesreau, New York Giants **1.96**
1913 AL Walter Johnson, Washington Senators **1.14**

RBIs
1920 NL George Kelly, New York Giants **94**
1920 AL Babe Ruth, New York Yankees **137**

SAVES
1969 NL Fred Gladding, Houston Astros **29**
1969 AL Ron Perranoski, Minnesota Twins **31**

Babe Ruth

GAME-WINNING RBIS
1980 NL Will Clark, San Francisco **18**
1980 AL Ken Singleton, Baltimore Orioles **19**

ON BASE PERCENTAGE
1985 NL Pedro Guerrero, Los Angeles Dodgers **.425**
1985 AL Wade Boggs, Boston Red Sox **.452**

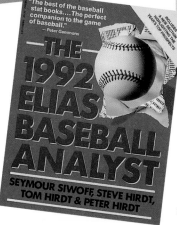

BY THE NUMBERS The Bill James Baseball Abstract *started out in 1977 as a self-published newsletter. However, its incisive team essays and opinionated player ratings made it a bestseller over the next 12 years. One competitor,* The Elias Baseball Analyst, *provided detailed situational breakdowns for every major leaguer. Another,* The National Pastime, *published by SABR, juxtaposes detailed statistical analyses with research pieces on the history of the game.*

How to read a **Box Score**

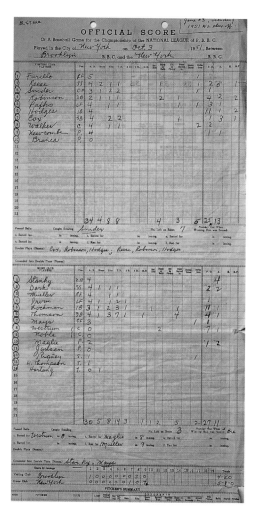

Box scores are to statistics as ore is to metal. They're the raw material of baseball's number fixation. At its simplest level, a box score can give you a quick morning rundown of who won and who lost yesterday. But that page of box scores in your sports section is really a low-tech time machine, a way to check out all 13 games that happened last night. It's a way to keep tabs on the bum your team traded away last spring. (Six earned runs in 2 1/3 innings! Yes!) Or the team that's sneaking up on you from behind. (Ouch, another shutout for Johnson.) Today's box scores are just one page in a bigger story that spans more than a hundred years. Every perfect game, every grand slam home run, and every oh-for-four with three strikeouts have been recorded somewhere. You may not want to go digging through all that newsprint, yet you can't help but sleep better knowing it's there.

OLD SCORECARD *Detailed scorekeeping and copious statistics helped convince the public that early baseball was a serious and systematic pursuit and not just a child's game.*

August 21, 1995: One Game

Here's how *USA Today Baseball Weekly* presents its boxscores. Atlanta, on the way to its first World Series title, edges Houston, which was struggling to maintain a slim lead over Colorado in the Wild Card race.

GOOSE EGGS *Two former Cy Young Award winners—Doug Drabek and Tom Glavine—are locked in an old-fashioned pitcher's duel. Until the sixth.*

GOING, GOING, GONE *Fred McGriff changes the game with one swing. He's done that more than once; the 3-run homer is his 281st round-tripper.*

GOOD NIGHT *Ryan Klesko rips two doubles and a triple. He also gunned down Dave Magadan trying to stretch a single into a double.*

DH ANYONE? *Glavine stranded five men during his three at bats, while his bullpen pals haven't had a hit all year. The "Left On" column and the seasonal averages are recent box score innovations.*

ROOKIE MISTAKE *Chipper Jones is thrown out at second base. A relatively new addition to the box score, the caught steal is doubly damaging because it costs a team both a base runner and an out.*

IF AT FIRST *At least this night the Astros didn't miss MVP first baseman Jeff Bagwell much. His replacement, Dave Magadan went two for four with two RBIs.*

BAD NIGHT *Ricky Gutierrez commits two errors, including the game loser in the sixth, goes zero for two, and grounds into a double play.*

THE GOOD NEWS *Pinch hitter John Cangelosi singles for Drabek and scores in Houston's four-run sixth. The bad news: with Drabek in the clubhouse, the bullpen can't hold the lead.*

ENOUGH STUFF *Glavine didn't have his best stuff tonight—he surrendered eight hits in seven innings—but he gave up only one free pass, kept the ball on the ground (thirteen groundouts, four flyouts) and got some help from the defense with two double plays.*

TOUGH LOSS *Craig McMurtry throws only nine pitches, allows one hit, but gives up two unearned runs and gets tagged with the loss in his first major league decision.*

WHERE ARE THEY? *Houston fans may have been holding a grudge over the 1994 strike that cost them a shot at the playoffs. Or maybe they just really wanted to see that Murphy Brown rerun.*

ATLANTA 5
HOUSTON 4

```
Atlanta . . . . . . .  000  003  200 - 5
Houston . . . . . . .  000  004  000 - 4
```

ATLANTA	ab	r	h	bi	bb	so	lo	avg
Grissom cf	5	0	0	0	0	1	0	.255
Blauser ss	4	2	0	0	0	1	1	.217
Jones 3b	5	1	2	0	0	0	0	.274
McGriff 1b	4	1	2	3	0	1	0	.268
Justice rf	3	1	1	0	1	1	1	.272
Klesko lf	3	0	3	2	1	0	0	.319
Lopez c	4	0	1	0	0	0	2	.302
Lemke 2b	3	0	0	0	1	1	3	.236
Glavine p	3	0	0	0	0	1	5	.224
a-Smith ph	1	0	0	0	0	0	0	.267
McMichael p	0	0	0	0	0	0	0	.000
Wohlers p	0	0	0	0	0	0	0	.000
Totals	35	5	9	5	3	6	12	

a-grounded to first for Glavine in the 8th.
▶ **BATTING** — 2B: Klesko 2 (18, Drabek, Hartgraves); Jones (19, McMurtry). 3B: Klesko (2, Drabek). HR: McGriff (19, 6th inning off Drabek, 1 on, 1 out). RBI: McGriff 3 (69), Klesko 2 (44). 2-out RBI: Klesko. **Runners left in scoring position, 2 out:** Glavine 3, Lopez 1. **Team LOB:** 7.
▶ **BASERUNNING** — CS: Jones (5, 2nd base by Drabek/Eusebio).
▶ **FIELDING** — E: Blauser (11, ground ball). **Outfield assists:** Klesko (Magadan at 2nd base). DP: 2 (Glavine-Blauser-McGriff, Blauser-Lemke-McGriff).

HOUSTON	ab	r	h	bi	bb	so	lo	avg
Hunter cf	5	0	1	0	0	0	2	.325
Mouton lf	4	1	0	0	1	0	4	.263
Biggio 2b	4	0	1	0	0	0	2	.296
Bell rf	3	1	1	0	1	1	1	.329
Eusebio c	4	1	1	2	0	2	2	.323
Magadan 1b	4	0	2	2	0	1	2	.279
Shipley 3b	4	0	3	0	0	0	1	.263
Gutierrez ss	2	0	0	0	0	0	2	.222
c-Thompson ph	1	0	1	0	0	0	0	.204
Drabek p	1	0	0	0	0	1	0	.205
a-Cangelosi ph	1	1	1	0	0	0	0	.354
McMurtry p	0	0	0	0	0	0	0	.000
Hartgraves p	0	0	0	0	0	0	0	.000
b-Simms ph	1	0	0	0	0	0	0	.308
Veres p	0	0	0	0	0	0	0	.000
d-May ph	1	0	0	0	0	0	1	.278
Totals	35	4	11	4	2	5	17	

a-singled for Drabek in the 6th; b-flied to right for Hartgraves in the 7th; c-singled for Gutierrez in the 9th; d-hit into fielder's choice for Veres in the 9th.
▶ **BATTING** — 2B: Eusebio (21, Glavine); Shipley (7, Wohlers). S: Gutierrez. RBI: Eusebio 2 (48), Magadan 2 (30). 2-out RBI: Eusebio 2, Magadan 2. **Runners left in scoring position, 2 out:** Hunter 1, Magadan 2, Mouton 2. GIDP: Mouton, Gutierrez. **Team LOB:** 7.
▶ **BASERUNNING** — SB: Bell (26, 2nd base off Wohlers/Lopez).
▶ **FIELDING** — E: Gutierrez 2 (3, catch, ground ball). **Outfield assists:** Mouton (Justice at home).

PITCHING	ip	h	r	er	bb	so	hr	era
ATLANTA								
Glavine (W, 12-5)	7	8	4	0	1	3	0	2.94
McMichael (H, 15)	1/3	1	0	0	1	0	0	3.05
Wohlers (S, 18)	1 2/3	2	0	0	0	2	0	1.86
HOUSTON								
Drabek	6	7	3	3	2	5	1	4.73
McMurtry (L, 0-1; H, 1)	1/3	1	2	0	0	0	0	11.25
Hartgraves (BS, 1)	2/3	1	0	0	1	0	0	2.73
Veres	2	0	0	0	0	1	0	1.84

WP: Glavine. **IBB:** Lemke (by Drabek). **HBP:** Blauser (by Drabek). **Pitches-strikes:** Drabek 91-57; McMurtry 9-6; Hartgraves 12-6; Veres 22-14; Glavine 100-63; Wohlers 22-18. **Ground-fly balls:** Drabek 7-5; McMurtry 0-1; Hartgraves 1-0; Veres 2-3; Glavine 13-4; McMichael 0-1; Wohlers 2-1. **Batters faced:** Drabek 27; McMurtry 3; Hartgraves 3; Veres 6; Glavine 28; McMichael 3; Wohlers 7.
▶ **UMPIRES** — HP: Terry Tata. 1B: Gerry Davis. 2B: Wally Bell. 3B: Mike Winters.
▶ **GAME DATA** — T: 2:59. **Att:** 15,291. Indoors.

WILLIAM HOWARD TAFT *was the first president to throw out the first ball of the season on April 14, 1910, a tradition that the following presidents have continued: (from left) Franklin D. Roosevelt, Harry Truman, Dwight D. Eisenhower, John F. Kennedy, and Ronald Reagan. Taft's Vice President James Sherman fared less well that day. He was struck in the head by a foul ball by Frank Baker of the A's and was knocked unconscious.*

MICKEY MANTLE *hits a first inning home run in the annual Hall of Fame game, in which big leaguers grace Cooperstown's Doubleday Field, which (according to legend) was the site of the very first baseball game.*

The Ceremony *of baseball*

The story goes that President Taft—an extremely large man—was attending a game in 1910. In the middle of the seventh inning, Taft suddenly stood up from his seat. The entire crowd, assuming the President was leaving the ballpark, respectfully rose to its feet as well. But then Taft abruptly sat down again to enjoy the rest of the game. The crowd followed suit, and the tradition of the seventh inning stretch was born.

GAME HARDWARE *Charlie Gehringer was presented with this commemorative belt buckle (above) for his participation in the 1935 All-Star Game.*

IMMORTALITY *Babe Ruth's Hall of Fame plaque (above).*

Baseball doesn't need a seventh inning stretch. There's no reason to throw out a first pitch or sing the National Anthem before each game. Managers don't need to wear uniforms. It's pointless to run around the bases after hitting a homer, or to throw four pitches to intentionally walk a batter. Baseball may have switched from a game played during the day on grass to a night game played frequently on turf, but its traditions and little ceremonies remain. When the visitors make their third out in the top of the seventh and everyone around you instinctively rises to sing "Take Me Out To the Ballgame," you'll understand why these traditions endure.

NICKNAMES have always been a part of the game: Bob "Death to Flying Things" Ferguson (left), captained the Hartford Dark Blues in the 1870s. Other players with colorful nicknames include Dixie "The People's Cheerce" Walker, Hugh "Losing Pitcher" Mulcahy, Walt "No Neck" Williams, Hank "Bow Wow" Arft, Eddie "The Walking Man" Yost, Sammy "Babe Ruth's Legs" Byrd, and Joe "Ducky Wucky" Medwick.

RED SCHOENDIENST *dons sliding pants as he gets ready for base-running drills with the Milwaukee Braves in 1960.*

The rites of Spring

THE 1913 GIANTS *do some roadwork at their Marlin Springs, Texas spring training site, which was chosen by manager John McGraw for its curative mineral baths and remote location. The tradition of spring training is almost as old as baseball itself, with Boss Tweed's New York Mutuals going south to New Orleans for a training session in 1869.*

Forget the swallows in Capistrano. Nothing announces that winter's over like the beginning of spring training. The phrase "pitchers and catchers report" is a surer sign than any blooming crocus. For the ballplayer in his prime, secure in his place on the team, spring training is a leisurely time, drills in the morning, golf in the afternoon, a gradual warm-up for the long season ahead. But for the hopeful rookie looking to catch on with the big club, or the vet trying to hang on for one more year, it's a time of high anxiety. There are jobs to be won, impressions to be made. Every day that passes without a grim message to report to the manager's office is met with a silent prayer of thanks. But whether it's a transition or audition, those long days in Florida and Arizona never seem to last quite long enough and before you can say, "bunting drills" it's time for the trip north, and the games that count.

"Anyone who comes to spring training in February is, of course, an honorary old man. No one who is unwilling to smell, taste, see, touch, and feel as though for the first time or last belongs there."

—Thomas Boswell,
from How Life Imitates the World Series

"Teams go south every spring to cripple their players. In the old days, they only stayed a couple of weeks, and they couldn't get many of them hurt in that time, but nowadays they stay till they get them all hurt."
—Will Rogers

"We're going down. We're going down, and I have a lifetime .300 average to take with me. Do you?"

—Pete Rose,

to airplane seatmate Hal King in 1974

On the Road

I t's not easy being the road team. From airline food to hotel curfews to the crowd ganging up on you during the seventh inning stretch—it's never root, root, root for the visiting team; life is tough wearing those road grays. And things haven't gotten any easier. The West Coast road trip, with its three-hour time change and red-eye return flights, has been given its share of credit for the demise of the .400 hitter. Just how tough is life on the road? This century, away teams have a winning percentage of .457. Home teams are .543. Recordwise, that's roughly the difference between mediocre and legendary managers Vern Rapp and Sparky Anderson's career records.

TRAIN TRAVEL *The White Sox in 1910.*

The Dog Days

Here's how one team, the New York Yankees, spent the month of August, 1995.

NEW YORK: AUGUST 1-3
The Yankees host the Milwaukee Brewers, winning two of three games.

DETROIT: AUGUST 4-6
They travel to Detroit and take two of three from the Tigers.

NEW YORK: AUGUST 7-13
The Yanks play eight games in seven days at home, beating Baltimore in two of three before losing a three of five to Cleveland.

BOSTON: AUGUST 14-16
Yanks lose two of three to their arch-rivals, the Red Sox.

AUGUST 17
Travel day: the Yankees go from Boston to Los Angeles.

ANAHEIM: AUGUST 18-20
The Yanks win the first game but drop the next two against the Angels.

OAKLAND: AUGUST 21-23
Road woes continue as the As sweep the Yankees in three games.

SEATTLE: AUGUST 24-27
The Mariners take the first three games before the Yanks snap their eight-game losing streak in the series finale.

NEW YORK: AUGUST 28-31
After traveling back across the country, the Yanks lose a make-up game to the Kansas City Royals on the 28th before taking three straight from the Angels.

FOR THE MONTH, *the Yankees travelled over 8,200 miles and played 31 games in 31 days, winning 14 of them. They began the month in second place, 4 1/2 games behind Boston; by August's end they were still in second, but 14 1/2 games back.*

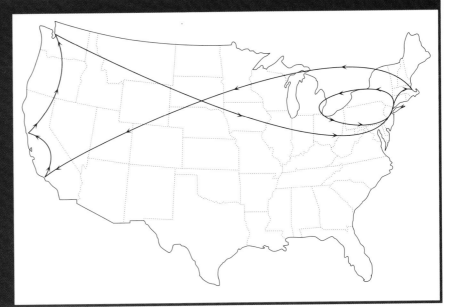

"When I made it to the majors, I was so relieved that my mode of transportation had improved. As I quickly discovered, a huge part of every major leaguers life is spent in the air. That's when he relaxes, or reflects about baseball, or makes attachments with other players—it's when teams come together."

—Tim McCarver

IRON HORSING AROUND *Lou Gehrig headed the Larrupin' Lous against the Bustin' Babes of Yankee teammate Babe Ruth in a post-World Series barnstorming tour in 1927. Gehrig, the 1927 MVP, (left) presents a $1,000 check to Pacific Coast League MVP Lefty O'Doul.*

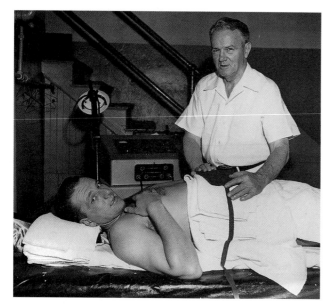

SPORTS MEDICINE *Pirates slugger Ralph Kiner gets diathermy treatment for his sore back from trainer Dr. Charles Jorgensen. Today, treatment for the same injury might include neuro-muscular stimulation, anti-inflammatory drugs, stretching exercises, and maybe even acupuncture.*

GUN HO *Dodger outfielder Pete Reiser was carried off the field on a stretcher 11 times in his career, once fracturing his skull running into the wall. Another time he was paralyzed for 10 days. The 1941 batting champion played more than 100 games a season only four times in his career.*

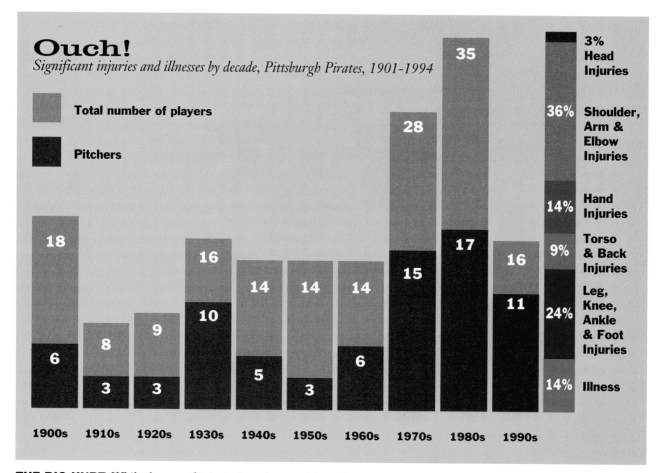

Ouch!
Significant injuries and illnesses by decade, Pittsburgh Pirates, 1901-1994

Total number of players

Pitchers

1900s: 18, 6
1910s: 8, 3
1920s: 9, 3
1930s: 16, 10
1940s: 14, 5
1950s: 14, 3
1960s: 14, 6
1970s: 28, 15
1980s: 35, 17
1990s: 16, 11

3% Head Injuries
36% Shoulder, Arm & Elbow Injuries
14% Hand Injuries
9% Torso & Back Injuries
24% Leg, Knee, Ankle & Foot Injuries
14% Illness

THE BIG HURT *While the rate of injuries have increased in real terms due to factors like Astroturf and hard on the arm pitches like the split finger fastball, there are other factors behind this apparent rise in time lost to injury. These days, players are less likely to play through a serious injury. And with the advent of sports medicine, many ailments like rotator cuff tears that once would have ended a career, can be treated and allow a player to come back after a stint on the disabled list.*

KOUFAX CALLS IT QUITS *In 1966, Dodger ace Sandy Koufax went 27-9 with a 1.73 ERA, winning his second consecutive Cy Young Award, but an arthritic elbow, diagnosed two years earlier, forced him to retire at the age of 31. That 1966 performance stands as the best ever by a pitcher in his final season, and in 1972, Koufax became the youngest player elected to the Hall of Fame.*

Baseball's Injuries

Most baseball injuries happen at home. Or within sixty feet six inches of it anyway. A pitcher will warm up patiently, ice his arm after games, wouldn't touch a suitcase on a bet, and yet if he stays around long enough, he'll inevitably come down with a sore arm. Or worse. Tom Browning actually broke his arm in midpitch. As for the perils of catching, ask Ray Fosse. He was badly injured when he was bowled over by Pete Rose in an All-Star Game. And while an everyday player worries about running into walls or hamstring pulls, he really thinks twice when he's at the plate, with a 90-mph fastball hurtling toward him.

PATIENTS OF JOBE *Southpaw Tommy John (above) was the first pitcher to have his elbow reconstructed by Dr. Frank Jobe (left), who took a tendon from his right arm and moved it to his left. John would pitch 14 more years in the majors.*

The era of
Expansion

THE CONTINENTAL LEAGUE *headed by president Branch Rickey (above) was conceived as the first challenge to major league baseball since the Federal League in 1914. Though the CL was not successful, it caused the American League to add the Los Angeles Angels and Washington Senators in 1961, and the National League to add the Houston Colt .45s and New York Mets in 1962.*

For 50 years, baseball geography was a simple subject. The same old 16 teams played in the same old cities. But in the 1950s, times changed--television, airline travel, a migration West—and this modernizing of America signalled the end of the league's cozy East Coast configuration. Baseball expanded because it could, and because it had to. And in the best American fashion, this expansion has something for everyone. Marginal players like expansion because it opens up more job possibilities. Stars like it because they get to hit or pitch against guys who would have been in the minors the year before. The owners like it because of the franchise fees—$2 million in the 1961 expansion, $95 million in 1993 for the Colorado Rockies and Florida Marlins—that the new owners fork over.

THE NATS *When the original Senators moved to Minnesota and became the Twins, an expansion version went to Washington in 1961.*

WALTER O'MALLEY *moved the Dodgers (Sandy Koufax, above) to the West Coast in 1958 amid great fan uproar and the rival Giants followed suit, completing baseball's manifest destiny. In a move that was designed to prevent more franchise shifts and head off a threat by the Continental League, expansion franchises were awarded to Los Angeles in 1961 and New York in 1962.*

1940 Census figures

IN 1950, *St. Louis was the westernmost major league city, and five cities—Philadelphia, Boston, New York, St. Louis and Chicago—had two or more major league teams. In 1995, 12 of the 26 U.S.-based teams were located west of the Mississippi, with the Arizona Diamondbacks scheduled to begin play in 1998.*

KEY
⬤ *Cities with 500,000 or more people*
✪
★ } *Major League Franchises*

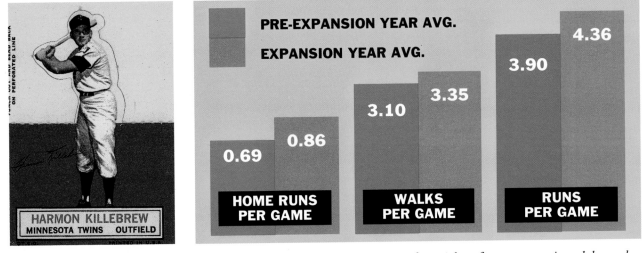

HARMON KILLEBREW *is one of 24 players to hit more than 40 home runs in an expansion year.*

PRE-EXPANSION YEAR AVG.

EXPANSION YEAR AVG.

0.69	0.86	
HOME RUNS PER GAME		

3.10	3.35
WALKS PER GAME	

3.90	4.36
RUNS PER GAME	

EXPANSION PITCHING *The expansion from eight to fourteen teams in each league has resulted in a dilution of pitching talent. The average expansion year results in increases of 8% in walks, 12% in runs scored, and 25% in homers over the preceding season.*

ROAD TRIP *In the 1880s Albert Spalding took a baseball team on a goodwill tour to places like Egypt and India, attempting to spread the game. In 1937 Dominican dictator Rafael Trujillo was determined to avenge an embarrassing loss for his namesake team, so he imported a Negro League All-Star team (above) that included Satchel Paige, Cool Papa Bell, and Josh Gibson. They were paid $30,000 for eight weeks work and suffered no racial discrimination, but they were escorted everywhere by armed guards, and when they were down in the seventh inning of the championship game, the assembled military began fingering their weapons. The Negro Leaguers quickly rallied and made a hasty getaway.*

Around the World

Baseball may be America's national pastime, but that hasn't kept it from spreading beyond our borders. Latin America is the home to winter leagues, where major leaguers hone their skills, and little towns like San Pedro de Macoris, where big league shortstops seem to grow on trees. Canadians will remember that Jackie Robinson was playing for the Montreal Royals when he broke the color barrier and that the Blue Jays won the first World Series played at least in part outside of the United States. Japan has combined samurai-like discipline with football-crowd fanaticism for a wholly unique brand of baseball. Kids in Taiwan and Korea have adopted the sport so completely that they regularly beat American Little Leaguers at their own game. And when baseball became an Olympic sport in 1984, the Russians even took up the game. Guess it's just hard to keep something this good a secret.

EL BEISBOL *Winter leagues played in the Carribean and Venezuela include many young and rehabbing major leaguers. Willie Mays (above left) wore the uniform of Santurce in Puerto Rico in the 1950s. Cuban leader Fidel Castro, (left) was a major league pitching prospect in his youth, and made the country a world power in amateur baseball.*

Baseball crazy **Japan**

ON A RAINY 1934 TOUR *of Japan, Babe Ruth played the outfield with an umbrella, while fellow All-Star Lou Gehrig wore galoshes at first. The Yankee teammates were two of the strikeout victims of teenager Eiji Sawamura, who came close to getting the hosts a win but lost 1-0.*

The strike zone is a little bigger. The ball is a little smaller. The crowds cheer from the first pitch to the last. Teams are named after their corporate owners. A tie is a good thing because nobody loses face. Welcome to baseball, Japanese style. It's hard to believe, but the Japanese take baseball even more seriously than we do. But Americans are now taking Japanese baseball more seriously, too. Internationalists will note that Sadaharu Oh, not Hank Aaron, owns the all-time home run record of 868. And whereas Japan was once the refuge of major league has-beens looking for one last paycheck, Cecil Fielder changed that when he returned stateside after playing in Japan and hit 50 homers. Other prime-time gaijin also made the trans-Pacific move. And if there was any doubt, seeing Hideo Nomo come to the Dodgers and strike out batters at a Ryanesque pace convinced Americans that Japan is also the land of the rising fastball.

BEFORE RIPKEN *Sachio Kinugasa, a first baseman for the Hiroshima Carp, was the first to break Lou Gehrig's consecutive games streak, stringing together 2,215 appearances. Other Japanese legends include Masaichi Kaneda was Japan's Walter Johnson, winning 400 games for the weak Yakult Swallows, and Yutaka Fukumoto who stole 1,065 bases, breaking Lou Brock's record.*

週刊 **読売スポーツ**

40円

特集

三冠王でどれだけかせぐ

9月25日号

PEANUTS AND FUGU *The rabidly excited fans in Japan eat sushi instead of hot dogs, throw foul balls back, and have cheering sections complete with drums, trumpets and team songs.*

Other games of
Ball

Although many have claimed otherwise, baseball wasn't born; it evolved—from cricket and children's games like town ball and rounders. And the evolution of bat-and-ball games didn't stop once the bases were set at 90 feet. Softball arose as a small-space 10-man alternative to baseball, and it subsequently splintered into slow-pitch, fast-pitch, high-arc, low-arc, and 12- and 16-inch variations. City kids adapted baseball to the street, with broomsticks for bats, rubber Spaldeens replacing the horsehide, and sewers doubling as bases. And Wiffle ball, the official plastic bat-and-ball game of America's backyards, is the only one where you don't mind getting hit by the pitch. But whatever baseball offshoot you play, there's nothing like the thrill of getting good wood . . . or aluminum . . . or plastic . . . on the ball.

"When I made the high school varsity, Ellen still had the best arm in the family."

—Cal Ripken Jr. *on his softball playing sister*

CRICKET, *which is played primarily in England and former English colonies like India and New Zealand, shares baseball's pastoral aesthetic and leisurely pace. Scoring often runs into the hundreds, and games can last for several days.*

FOUR SEWERS OR BUST

On his off days, the young Willie Mays (above) could sometimes be found playing stickball in the Bronx, taking his hacks with a broomstick instead of a Louisville Slugger. Softball comes in many flavors—fast-pitch, in which hurlers can top 90 mph; slow-pitch, which is the staple of after-work leagues, and 16-inch, a Chicagoland specialty, which is played with a giant ball caught without the benefit of a glove.

THE BEAT REPORTER • PHOTOGRAPHERS OVER THE AIRWAVES • VENDORS AND CLOWNS • FANS • THE COLLECTING MANIA

Chapter Six

It's a sad fact of life that we can't all be good enough to play major league baseball. But we can sell hot dogs, rip tickets, take photos, play the organ, chase foul balls, or dress up in a chicken suit. Anything to be a part of the game we love. Baseball could certainly exist without its extensive support system, but why would it ever want to? The people who do their jobs outside the white lines are also a part of baseball's enduring appeal.

Clockwise from top left: San Francisco batboy, 1990; opening day crowd from 1938; an array of baseball cards; a press pass; photographers capture a Babe Ruth moment, 1942; Grantland Rice.

Grantland Rice

Behind the Scenes

The Press

Just as the game changed so dramatically in the 20th century, so has the role of the newspaper reporters who cover the game—the "beat" writers. Once, they carefully described every play in flowery detail. Today, it is no longer necessary. Fans who weren't at the ballpark probably saw the entire game on TV or caught highlights on the news. Articles in tomorrow's paper must probe more deeply. Why is Joe Homer in a slump? What are the team's chances of signing a top free agent? When is Skip Manager going to get canned? Previously, beat writers viewed themselves as the promotional arm of the team. In the post-Watergate era, reporters see their jobs as a search for the truth. And the truth, of course, isn't always pretty.

TOOLS OF THE TRADE *for the reporters of yesteryear. Above is the typewriter used by Ken Smith, who covered the Giants for 30 years until they moved to San Francisco and the camera used by the* Philadelphia Inquirer *photographer Robert C. Moon in the 1940s. Covering today's night games, beat reporters rush to write their stories on laptop computers while the game is still in progress and transmit copy by modem to their editors in order to meet the deadline for a morning paper.*

"Sportswriting is the most pleasant way of making a living that man has yet devised."

—Red Smith

PHOTOGRAPHERS *used to get close to the action by bringing bulky Speed Graphic cameras onto the field. "The cameraman was in constant danger from hard-hit drives," wrote photographer Charles M. Conlon. "I was seriously injured twice. On one occasion, less than half an hour after I had assisted in caring for a brother photographer who was hit in the head by a batted ball, a vicious drive down the first base line caught me just above the ankle, and I was unable to walk for a couple of weeks."*

UNTIL THE 1890s *most newspapers did not cover sports, so specialized publications appeared. The Sporting News printed its first weekly issue on March 17, 1886, and became "the Bible of Baseball." Until radio came along in the 1920s, newspaper accounts of baseball games were long, detailed, and colorfully descriptive.*

GRANTLAND RICE *(left) set the standard for polished and poetic sports writing from the roaring '20s through World War II. Rice coined the most memorable sports saying ever, "It's not whether you win or lose, it's how you play the game." World Series press pins (right) served as credentials for the media.*

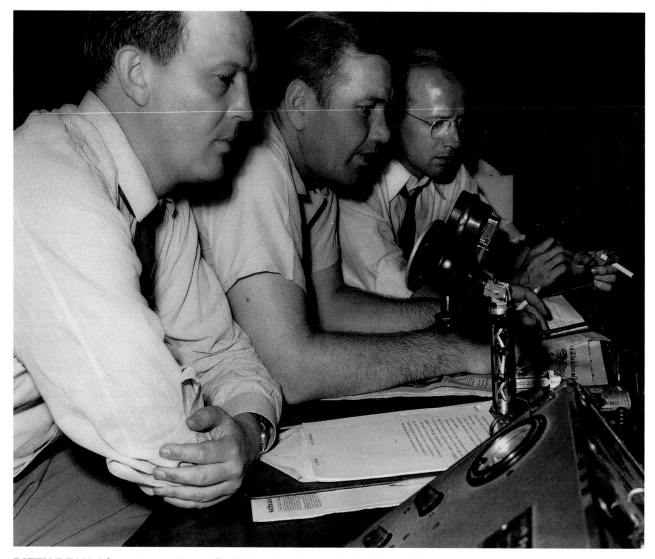

DIZZY DEAN *(above, in center) gave English teachers fits in the 1940s by talking about players with "testicle fortitude" who "slud into third" on WIL in St. Louis and later on CBS-TV. But Dean's fractured grammar and inimitable style had millions of fans riveted to their radios.*

VOICES OF NEW YORK *Bob Murphy (on left) has been the voice of the Mets since their start in 1962 and Yankee Phil Rizzuto (on right) jumped into the broadcast booth when he retired as a player in 1956, staying there until 1995.*

IT SEEMS WEIRD *for fans to bring their radios to the ballpark, but many want to listen to their favorite announcer's play-by-play and analysis. Fans have even been spotted with portable TV sets on their laps. When the camera picks them up, they see themselves watching TV on their own screens.*

Over the Airwaves

From ticker tapes to computers, the media have always used the available technology of the day to tell the world about the game. In 1869, 25 years after Samuel Morse tapped out the words "What hath God wrought!" Harry M. Millar of the Cincinnati Commercial began telegraphing instant reports about the Cincinnati Red Stockings to his paper. The telegraph was used to re-create games even after August 5, 1921, when a major league baseball game was broadcast by radio for the first time (the Pirates beat the Phillies, 8-5, at Forbes Field). Televised baseball began on May 17, 1939, with a college game between Columbia and Princeton. Three months later a game between the Dodgers and Reds was televised from Ebbets Field. Today, fans can get play-by-play accounts of games through online information services and the Internet.

RADIO *given to the 1940 Reds for winning the World Series.*

With each new technological advance, many team owners worried that fans wouldn't come to see games at the ballpark if they could experience them in the comfort of their homes. In fact, the opposite has always proven to be true. The more baseball people got by wire and airwave, the more they were interested in the sport and the more they came to see games in person.

BATBOYS *don't just carry bats. They also sort the players' mail and laundry, run their errands, get their food, shine their shoes, and sweep the clubhouse. They don't get paid much, but the fringe benefits are terrific: watching the game from the dugout, helping warm up the players, and taking home cool souvenirs like cracked bats and torn jerseys. Most of all, they get to meet and hang out with their heroes. Some batboys (such as Steve Garvey and Jim Lefebvre) even went on to become big-league ballplayers themselves.*

CLOWNS *such as Max Patkin (left) have entertained fans since the early 1900s. Patkin was a former minor league pitcher who became a star when he switched to performing gangly pantomimes on the foul lines to entertain fans. "The clown prince of baseball," as he was known, was seen in the movie* Bull Durham.

VENDORS *get in free and they have a great view of the game, but they have to stand the whole time and face the wrong way, such as the young man (left) hawking Cokes at Ebbets Field.*

MASCOTS *started out as good luck charms for teams and later became entertainment for the fans. Typically, when the home team hit a homer, the mascot would pop out and do something amusing like flap its wings (St. Louis's Busch Eagle), do a dance (Atlanta's Chief Nok-A-Homa), or slide into a mug of beer (Milwaukee's Bernie Brewer). The San Diego Chicken and Phillie Phanatic (right, with Pete Rose) perform elaborate routines and have become stars in their own right.*

Familiar **Figures**

While some sports feature continuous action, in baseball, it comes in short bursts. Between pitches there is plenty of time to scope out the stands, grab a snack, check the out of town scores, maybe take a walk to see what the view is like from behind the plate. Along the way you're likely to encounter a cast of characters that rivals the studio audience of a game show. In their small way, they help make baseball what it is.

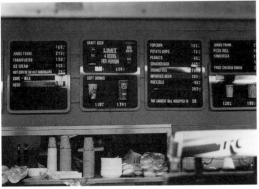

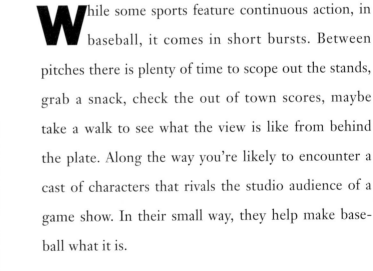

HOT DOGS *always taste better at the ballpark, maybe because they were invented there. Legend has it that one chilly summer day in 1901 at the Polo Grounds, vendor Harry M. Stevens wasn't selling much ice cream. The park was located in a German neighborhood, so Stevens sent out for some small wursts. He slipped them in rolls so fans would be able to hold them without burning their hands, getting messy, or needing plates or utensils. The wursts were known as "dachshunds" and the snack came to be called the hot dog.*

The Fans

You only hear about the quirky fans, such as Hilda Chester, the Brooklyn soup saleslady who rang a cowbell and passed notes to Leo Durocher in Ebbets Field. Or Wild Bill Hagy, the Baltimore taxi driver who would climb up on the dugout where he would twist his body around to spell O-R-I-O-L-E-S.

But most baseball fans don't come to the ballpark to perform; they come to watch the game. True fans are well informed and love to discuss the hit-and-run, the double switch, the infield fly rule, and other intricacies of the game. They don't just watch the ball; they watch the fielders, the runner taking his lead, the third base coach flashing signs. They know to cheer when a batter bounces out to first but advances the runner. They know to boo when a double play ball only results in a single out. The most knowledgeable fans are often found in the farthest reaches of the bleachers, carefully recording each play on their scorecards. All fans, of course, feel that they know what is the right strategy for their team, and they're not afraid to let their feelings be known.

"Then from 5,000 throats and
*   more there rose a lusty yell;*
It rumbled through the valley, it
*   rattled in the dell;*
It knocked upon the mountain and
*   recoiled upon the flat,*
For Casey, mighty Casey, was
*   advancing to the bat."*

—Ernest L. Thayer

BOSTON FAN *Lolly Hopkins (above, at right) had been rooting for the Red Sox for 45 years when this picture was taken in 1955. That meant she was around to enjoy the Sox winning the World Series in 1912, 1915, 1916, and 1918. Lolly didn't know it then, but the Sox would go the next three-quarters of a century without winning another World Series. Today's Red Sox fans are still waiting for it. Chicago fans are even more patient. The White Sox haven't won since 1917, and the Cubs haven't won since 1908.*

"One of the chief duties of the fan is to engage in arguments with the man behind him."

—Robert Benchley

"If people don't want to come out to the ball park, nobody's going to stop them."

—Yogi Berra

The myth of **Attendance**

While some people say base-ball is a game whose glory years are long gone, attendance figures certainly don't back that up. In the "roaring twenties," which is considered baseball's golden age, not many people actually came out to the ballpark. The 1927 Yankees, for example, were one of the greatest teams ever. However, they only drew 1,164,015 fans that year, and most teams in the majors drew about half that number. During the Depression, attendance suffered terribly. The St. Louis Browns drew 80,922 people in the entire 1935 season and all the major league

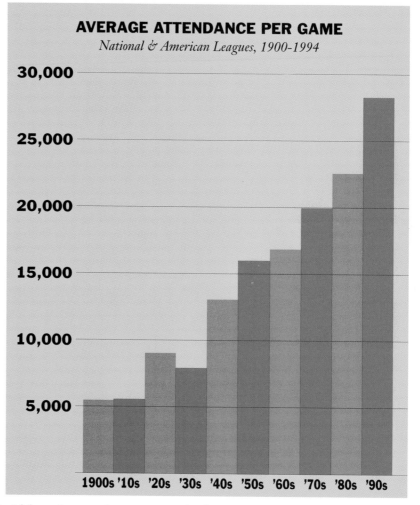

AVERAGE ATTENDANCE PER GAME
National & American Leagues, 1900-1994

teams drew only a total of 7,345,316. Although attendance zoomed when the soldiers came home from World War II, major league attendance nose-dived from 20 million to 14.4 million between 1948 and 1953.

By contrast, look at 1993. The Yankees, playing without heroes like Ruth and Gehrig, with 2,416,942 fans easily outdrew the 1927 Yankees. In fact, all 28 teams in 1993 topped the 1927 Yankees in attendance. Twenty-one teams topped two million, and seven topped *three* million. All told, more than 70 million tickets were sold to major league baseball games in 1993, over 10 times as many as in 1927. Furthermore, baseball now competes with pro football, basketball, TV, video games, and lots of other activities for a fan's spare time. While it's true that overall population increased between the 1920s and the 1990s, there can be no doubt that baseball is more popular now than it ever was.

ATTENDANCE *has climbed over the long term despite two World Wars, a major gambling scandal, competition from emerging professional sports, and technology that bring fans at home closer to the game than those in the ballpark. After the 1994 season, when the World Series was canceled due to a labor dispute, attendance took a major (20%) drop.*

A mania for Collecting

The first baseball cards were printed in 1886 by tobacco companies who wanted a marketing premium and needed something cheap and stiff to prevent their product from being crushed during shipping. Who would have thought little pieces of cardboard would some day be worth thousands of dollars and one of them (the Honus Wagner T-206) would sell for nearly half a million? Now, over a century after the first cards were printed, more than 10 million Americans are collecting cards, autographed balls, bats, jerseys, and other baseball memorabilia. Kids no longer put baseball cards into their bicycle spokes with clothespins—they put them in protective plastic pages. Mothers no longer haul shoeboxes full of cards out to the garbage—they haul them to card stores to be appraised. Card collecting started out as a hobby and became a billion-dollar business.

ROOKIEMANIA *A young collector with his Nolan Ryan rookie card, which was worth pennies when Ryan made his major league debut and worth over $1,000 by the time he retired. Cards of rookies who became stars are the most sought after by collectors. Mickey Mantle's rookie card is valued at over $25,000.*

Bibliography

Adair, Robert K. *The Physics of Baseball*. New York: HarperCollins, 1990.

Brancazio, Peter J. *Sport Science*. New York: Simon & Schuster, 1984.

Cluck, Bob. *Play Better Baseball*. Chicago: Contemporary Books, 1993.

Curran, William. *Strikeout: A Celebration of the Art of Pitching*. New York: Crown, 1995.

Dewan, John and Don Zminda. *STATS 1993 Baseball Scoreboard*. New York: HarperCollins, 1993.

Dickson, Paul. *Baseball's Greatest Quotations*. New York: HarperCollins, 1991.

Dickson, Paul. *The Dickson Baseball Dictionary*. New York: Avon Books, 1989.

Fiffer, Steve. *How to Watch Baseball*. New York: Facts On File, 1987.

Gershman, Michael. *Diamonds: The Evolution of the Ballpark*. Boston: Houghton Mifflin, 1993.

Gutman, Dan. *Banana Bats & Ding-Dong Balls*. New York: Macmillan, 1995.

Gutman, Dan. *Baseball Babylon*. New York: Penguin, 1992.

Gutman, Dan. *It Ain't Cheatin' If You Don't Get Caught*. New York: Penguin, 1990.

Helyar, John. *Lords of the Realm*. New York: Ballantine Books, 1994.

James, Bill. *The Baseball Abstract* (annual, 1981-1989). New York: Ballantine.

James, Bill. *The Baseball Book 1990*. New York: Villard, 1990.

James, Bill. *The Historical Baseball Abstract*. New York: Villard, 1986.

Kindall, Jerry. *Sports Illustrated Baseball: Play the Winning Way*. New York: Time Inc., 1988.

Lowry, Philip J. *Green Cathedrals*. Addison Wesley, 1992.

MacFarlane, Paul, editor. *Daguerreotypes*. St. Louis: The Sporting News, 1981.

McCabe, Neal and McCabe, Constance. *Baseball's Golden Age: The Photographs of Charles M. Conlon*. New York: Harry N. Abrams, 1993.

Neft, David and Richard Cohen. *The Sports Encyclopedia: Baseball*. New York: St. Martin's, 1995.

Quigley, Martin. *The Crooked Pitch: The Curveball in American Baseball History*. Chapel Hill, N.C.: Algonquin Books, 1984.

Schrier, Eric W. and Allman, William F. *Newton at the Bat: The Science in Sports*. New York: Scribner's, 1984.

Shannon, Bill and Kalinsky, George. *The Ballparks*. New York: Hawthorn Books, 1975.

Shatzkin, Mike, editor. *The Ballplayers: Baseball's Ultimate Biographical Reference*. New York: Morrow, 1990.

Siwoff, Seymour, Steve Hirdt, et al. *The Baseball Analyst* (annual). New York: Collier.

Sullivan, Dean A. *Early Innings: A documentary history of Baseball, 1825-1908*. Lincoln: University of Nebraska Press, 1995.

The Baseball Encyclopedia. New York: Macmillan.

The Baseball Register. St. Louis: The Sporting News Publishing Co., 1995.

The Baseball Research Journal (annual). Cleveland: SABR.

The Scouting Report: 1995. HarperCollins, 1995.

Thorn, John, and Holway, John. *The Pitcher*. Englewood Cliffs, N.J.: Prentice Hall, 1987.

Thorn, John and Pete Palmer, editors. *Total Baseball*. New York: Warner Books, 1995.

USA Today's Baseball Weekly.

Vickery, A. Lou. *Answers to Baseball's Most Asked Questions*. Indianapolis: Masters Press, 1995.

Williams, Ted, and Underwood, John. *The Science of Hitting*. New York: Simon & Schuster, 1970.

Zoss, Joel and Bowman, John. *Diamonds in the Rough: The Untold History of Baseball*. New York: Macmillan, 1989.

Photo Credits

Frontmatter:
National Baseball Library & Archive, Cooperstown, NY—I, II, V, VI, VII.

Introduction:
National Baseball Library & Archive, Cooperstown, NY—1, 2, 3, 4, 5, 6, 7.
Walker, Richard—5.

Chapter One:
Associated Press/Wide World Photos—13, 25, 28, 32, 39.
Courtesy of Jeff Christensen—9, 12, 15, 24, 26, 34, 36, 40, 42.
Courtesy of Easton Sports, Inc.—20, 21.
Focus on Sports—18, 35, 36, 37, 38, 44.
Courtesy of Hillerich & Bradsby/©1994 Earl Fansler Photography, Inc.—16, 17, 20, 21.
Andy Jurinko, courtesy of Gallery Henoch, New York—15.
Litwhiler, Danny—42.
National Baseball Library & Archive, Cooperstown, NY—8, 10, 13, 14, 15, 16, 17, 18, 19, 21, 24, 26, 27, 29, 30, 33, 34, 36, 37, 38, 39, 40, 41, 42.
Rauhofer, Victoria—11, 12, 22.
Rawlings—11, 23.
Stewart, Milo Jr./National Baseball Library & Archive, Cooperstown, NY—24.
UPI/Bettman—9, 12, 30, 31, 35, 45.
Walker, Richard—8, 9, 10, 12, 13, 18, 20, 22, 25, 26, 29, 30, 31, 32, 33, 34, 37, 38, 44.
Zimmerman, Tom/National Baseball Library & Archive, Cooperstown, NY—40.

Chapter Two:
Associated Press/Wide World Photo—54, 65, 66, 69.
Courtesy of Jeff Christensen—47, 62.
Delta Imaging—48, 49, 52, 57, 59, 60, 61.
Focus on Sports—46, 47, 48, 50, 51, 55, 56, 67, 68.
Grimwade, John—49.
©The Harold E. Edgerton 1992 Trust, courtesy of Palm Press, Inc.—59.
National Baseball Library & Archive, Cooperstown, NY—46, 49, 53, 55, 58, 60, 61, 62, 63, 64, 65, 66, 67, 68.
PhotoFile—56.
Toronto Star/David Cooper—69.
UPI/Bettman—55, 56, 68, 69.
Walker, Richard—61.
Weir, Christopher—69.

Chapter Three:
Associated Press/ Wide World Photos—83, 93, 95, 96, 99, 104, 105, 108, 119, 124, 127.
Chicago Sun Times—117.
Courtesy of Jeff Christensen—105, 121.
Daily Democrat—105.
Delta Imaging—90.
Duryea, Drix/National Baseball Library & Archive, Cooperstown, NY—78.
Focus on Sports—70, 72, 73, 80, 81, 84, 88, 89, 91, 92, 95, 96, 100, 106, 111, 114, 115, 116, 117, 119, 121, 122.
George I. Browne Photography/National Baseball Library & Archive, Cooperstown, NY—85.
Andy Jurinko, courtesy of Gallery Henoch, New York—75.
Kuhns, Pete—84.
National Baseball Library & Archive, Cooperstown, NY—70, 71, 77, 79, 81, 82, 83, 84, 85, 86, 88, 91, 93, 94, 95, 96, 97, 98, 99, 100, 101, 102, 104, 105, 107, 108, 109, 110, 111, 112, 113, 114, 115, 116, 117, 118, 119, 121, 122, 125, 126, 127, 128, 129.

Rawlings—117.

Rucki, Mike/National Baseball Library & Archive, Cooperstown, NY—79.

Toronto Star/Dave Cooper—85; John Mahler—104.

UPI/Bettman—71, 72, 76, 77, 82, 85, 88, 90, 96, 97, 99, 100, 104, 107, 113, 116, 120.

Walker, Richard—71, 74-75, 77, 78, 98, 104, 111.

Weir, Christopher—101, 112.

Chapter Four:

Associated Press/ Wide World Photos—138, 141, 154.

Courtesy of AstroTurf®—143, 144.

Courtesy of Jeff Christensen—130, 131, 142, 147, 152.

Courtesy of the Cleveland Indians/Sue Ogrocki—131, 154.

Focus on Sports—157.

Courtesy of Hellmuth, Obata & Kassabaum—150.

Andy Jurinko, courtesy of Gallery Henoch, New York—136, 139.

National Baseball Library & Archive, Cooperstown, NY—130, 131, 132, 133, 134, 135, 136, 137, 138, 141, 142, 147, 152, 153, 155, 156, 157.

Plain Dealer—150.

RAN International—131, 148, 149.

Stewart, Milo Jr./National Baseball Library & Archive, Cooperstown, NY—150.

Toronto Star/Jeff Goode—155.

UPI/Bettman—131, 146.

Walker, Richard—130, 133, 136, 137, 138, 146, 153, 156.

Zimmerman, Tom/National Baseball Library & Archive, Cooperstown, NY—155, 157.

Chapter Five:

Archive Photos—194, 195.

Associated Press/World Wide Photos—158, 160, 161, 163, 164, 168, 171, 173, 177, 178, 185, 186, 187, 188, 189, 192.

Courtesy of Jeff Christensen—159, 163, 166, 172, 178, 179, 181, 190, 191, 193.

Focus on Sports—173, 175, 178, 179.

Courtesy of Dr. Jobe's Office—189.

National Baseball Library & Archive, Cooperstown, NY—158, 159, 160, 161, 162, 163, 164, 165, 166, 167, 168, 169, 170, 171, 172, 173, 176, 177, 178, 179, 180, 182, 184, 185, 186, 190 192, 193, 195.

PhotoFile—161, 177.

UPI/Bettman—162, 168, 169, 183, 185, 190.

Walker, Richard—174, 180, 183, 193, 194.

Washington Post/Arthur Ellis—182.

Weir, Christopher—187, 191.

Chapter Six:

Associated Press/Wide World Photos—197, 200, 205, 207.

© Barry, David—196, 202.

Courtesy of the Baseball Writers Association of America, New York Chapter—200.

Chicago Sun Times—207.

Courtesy of Jeff Christensen—197.

Focus on Sports—203, 204.

National Baseball Library & Archive, Cooperstown, NY—196, 197, 199, 200, 202, 203, 204, 205.

Plain Dealer—201.

Rauhafer, Victoria—199.

Rochster Times Union/Lloyd E. Klos—202.

UPI/Bettman Archives—199.

Walker, Richard—197, 198, 199, 201, 207.

Index

About the author

Dan Gutman is the author of numerous books about baseball, including *It Ain't Cheatin' If You Don't Get Caught, Baseball Babylon, Baseball's Biggest Bloopers, World Series Classics, Baseball's Greatest Games,* and *Banana Bats & Ding-Dong Balls*. He lives in Haddonfield, New Jersey, with his wife, Nina, and his children, Sam and Emma.

Tim McCarver spent twenty-one years as a major league catcher, first with the St. Louis Cardinals and then with the Philadelphia Phillies. Today one the game's most highly respected broadcasters and analysts, he is also the author of *Oh Baby, I Love It*. He lives in Gladwyne, Pennsylvania.